First published in the United States of America in 2008 by
UNIVERSE PUBLISHING A Division of Rizzoli International Publications, Inc.
300 Park Avenue South, New York, NY 10010
www.rizzoliusa.com

© 2008 by the International Tennis Federation

2008 2009 2010 / 10 9 8 7 6 5 4 3 2 1

Designed by Domino 4 Limited, Weybridge, United Kingdom
Printed in England

ISBN 13: 978-0-7893-1689-9

CONTENTS

PRESIDENT'S MESSAGE

IN 1900 AMERICAN DWIGHT DAVIS DONATED A SILVER CUP AS A PRIZE FOR A NEW COMPETITION that sought to foster international understanding among nations through tennis. More than 107 years later, that cup and the competition that now bears his name remain an influential and unifying force in a world that is often divided by conflict and confusion. Today teams from all over the world, more than 130 countries, compete against each other for the honor and privilege of representing their country and a chance to win the Davis Cup, which now sits on three very large plinths containing the names of the top nations and players who have battled so valiantly for this trophy.

One of the first names to be carved into the trophy was that of Davis himself, who competed in the first competition in 1900 and was part of the team that won a first of what is now thirty-two titles for the United States.

In 2007 the United States Davis Cup team ended a twelve-year title drought with a comprehensive 4–1 victory over Russia in Portland, Oregon. More than twelve thousand fans came each day to the Memorial Coliseum to watch Andy Roddick, James Blake, Bob and Mike Bryan, and their captain, Patrick McEnroe, complete a seven-year quest to win the Cup. The atmosphere was spectacular throughout the weekend but, when the Bryans closed it out on Saturday, the celebrations were especially emotional and dramatic with the team and their supporters close to tears. This victory in front of a joyous home crowd justified this team's hard work and sacrifice and made the difficult times seem very far away.

Last year was another excellent year for Davis Cup by BNP Paribas, with more than 550,000 people attending ties around the world, including a spectacular World Group Play-off Round that featured players of the caliber of Roger Federer, Novak Djokovic, Tomas Berdych, and Andy Murray and attracted enormous crowds, including the largest Play-off round in history with more than twenty thousand a day in Serbia. We added a new high-profile sponsor in Rolex and renewed our longstanding sponsorship with Hugo Boss through 2012. The reach of this competition through our television and web audiences continues to grow unabated.

I want to thank Chris Bowers, who has written another wonderful volume, bringing to life the Davis Cup story of 2007. His meticulous research and passion for the competition eloquently ensures the reader a complete understanding of how this year's Davis Cup by BNP Paribas has evolved. I would also like to thank the photographers whose images so beautifully illustrate this book, our magazines, and our websites.

This book celebrates the nations and the players who contested the Davis Cup by BNP Paribas in 2007. They delighted the spectators who were lucky enough to be present, television audiences around the world, and the enormous web audience who followed every point on daviscup.com.

Congratulations again to the United States on their victory, and we look forward to another great year of Davis Cup by BNP Paribas in 2008.

Francesco Ricci Bitti
President, International Tennis Federation

BNP PARIBAS

Giving tennis the advantage

SPONSOR OF TENNIS
EVERY KIND OF TENNIS

FOR MORE THAN 34 YEARS, BNP PARIBAS, one of the world's foremost banking groups and the number one bank in the euro zone, has chosen to support tennis.

Together with its 155,000 employees in more than 85 countries, BNP Paribas shares a number of core values with the sport, most notably enthusiasm associated with a sense of discipline, performance allied with fair play, and a desire for recognition combined with a sense of tradition and elegance.

As the sponsor of "every kind of tennis," BNP Paribas:

- Encourages junior tennis through its support of Junior Fed Cup by BNP Paribas, the BNP Paribas Cup (in conjunction with UNESCO) and Junior Davis Cup by BNP Paribas ;
- Provides substantial assistance in several of the countries in which the bank is present for educational tennis programmes developed by national associations for amateur players of all ages ;
- Supports sports out-reach programmes such as "Fête le Mur", a charitable organisation founded by Yannick Noah, which aims to promote social cohesion in underprivileged areas of France by involving disadvantaged youngsters in playing tennis ;
- Actively involved in wheelchair tennis as the title sponsor of the "BNP Paribas Open de France", the Roland Garros of the discipline ;
- Partners tennis at a worldwide level through its close association with numerous elite tennis events – the French Open since 1973, the BNP Paribas Masters in Paris, the Monte Carlo TMS event, the Bank of the West Classic in California (Bank of the West is a BNP Paribas Company) and the Rome Masters Series event which in 2007 became the "Internazionai BNL d'Italia" following the integration of Banca Nazionale del Lavoro (BNL, the 6th largest bank in Italy) into the BNP Paribas Group in 2006 making Italy its second biggest domestic market ;
- Since 2001, has been a proud member of the ITF family, sponsoring the world's largest international team competitions for both men and women : Davis Cup by BNP Paribas and Fed Cup by BNP Paribas.

The Group's steadfast commitment to tennis and its wide-ranging, yet coherent and balanced, programme of sponsorship, reflects the spirit in which BNP Paribas builds relationships with each and every customer. In much the same way, this year's champions from the United States have remained faithful to their cause and deservedly won their place in history despite some setbacks along the way. A well balanced unit, strong in both singles and doubles, their victory is testament to the power of teamwork and mirrors BNP Paribas' collaboration with its sister company, Bank of the West, in creating a highly successful hospitality programme for the 2007 final. Once again we have greatly enjoyed the Davis Cup by BNP Paribas year and hope that you will enjoy reliving it with us through this magnificent book.

Michel Pébereau

Michel Pébereau
Chairman, BNP Paribas

FOREWORD

FIFTEEN YEARS AGO, I ATTENDED THE 1992 DAVIS CUP FINAL. The U.S. won with possibly the greatest Davis Cup team ever: Andre Agassi, Jim Courier, Pete Sampras, and John McEnroe—and Sampras didn't even play singles. I was ten years old and the event changed my life and the way I viewed tennis. I never would have imagined that I would someday get to play Davis Cup for the United States.

Every time I play Davis Cup it is surreal. Because of that final, I have always been excited about Davis Cup. It has always been a huge priority for me. Being part of a winning Davis Cup team has been a goal of mine since I started playing. I was not one of those kids raised to be a tennis player at all. But that was pretty powerful, to be with other fans in an arena like that, seeing your heroes play and hearing the national anthem played for the first time. I fell in love with Davis Cup then.

It has been a few days since we won the Davis Cup, and I have been asked a lot how this compares to anything I have achieved in tennis. To bring the Cup back to the United States is an amazing feeling. But more important, to share this journey with my teammates has been so much fun and an honor.

You cannot win Davis Cup alone; you need a team effort. To be a part of a team is unique in tennis. You are playing for more than yourself. You are playing for the guys on your bench as much as you are for your country. The highs you experience are higher and the lows are lower. During my seven years playing Davis Cup (it's hard to believe I have been playing Davis Cup for that long), I have had a ton of memories, both good and bad, so to celebrate this win at home in front of more than twelve thousand of the most patriotic fans in the world—including my parents and two brothers—was amazing.

Throughout my Davis Cup career, I have been fortunate to have some of my best friends as my teammates. I have become really close to James, Bob, and Mike these past few years. Sure, we have shared the common goal of winning the Davis Cup, but there is nothing that can bring a group of guys together like being in a foreign country, playing against a full house of fans cheering against you and the only friendly faces in the building are your teammates on the bench. Davis Cup weeks are among my favorite weeks of the season.

I am so happy that Mardy Fish and Robby Ginepri were in Portland to help us prepare for the final. They are as much a part of this win as the four of us who played. Mardy may be the highest ranked practice partner in the history of Davis Cup, and Robby worked hard to make sure we were ready for the Russians. That needs to be acknowledged. It is also what makes our win special, that we were all here together. Winning Davis Cup is not an annual endeavor. It is a process, and everyone has been involved.

Each year this book tells the story of the Davis Cup competition. Our run to the title this year, though, extends beyond 2007. Probably the most pivotal year was 2005, when we had a tough home loss to Croatia in the first round, then had to travel to Belgium for the World Group Play-off on clay. The win in Belgium was the first time that James, Bob, Mike, and I played together. Since then we have played eight straight ties together—a record for the U.S. Davis Cup team—and we have become a team in every sense of the word. We have shared a lot of laughs. These guys are like my brothers.

It also meant a lot for us to win the Davis Cup for our captain, Patrick McEnroe. His first tie as captain was my first tie as a player. He has been there for me and this team from the start, and it is an honor to have taken this entire journey with him at the helm.

Finally, I would like to thank the USTA for their support of Davis Cup. They put a lot of time and resources to making sure we have everything we need at home and on the road. They put on a great show at the Final and work hard to make sure each home tie is something the players and the fans enjoy.

I hope you enjoy this look back at the 2007 Davis Cup. It is something that I will always treasure.

Andy Roddick

INTRODUCTION

CAUSE AND EFFECT ARE NOT ALWAYS EASY TO SEE. It's often obvious if the effect immediately follows the cause, but sometimes the time lag between action and effect can be a long one. Like fifteen years.

In the first week of December 1992, Blanche Roddick took her tennis-loving sons, Lawrence and Andy, to the Tarrant County Center in Fort Worth, near Dallas, where the Davis Cup final was being staged. They were among a group of thirty-or-so tennis players from the Courtyard Tennis Club in Austin, Texas, who got their tickets through the USTA. In the tennis world at large in 1992, and even in American tennis circles, the final was nothing new. The USA had been in the final the previous two years and had won in 1990 inside two days. And the Fort Worth arena had a capacity of barely more than five thousand. But something important happened that day that would affect the future. Young Andy Roddick saw a side to tennis he hadn't experienced until then—the cheering, the team camaraderie, the sense of playing for one's country. And he wanted to be part of it.

Tennis players are asked to do a fair bit of off-court work: autograph sessions, coaching clinics, pro-am events, and the like. It comes with the territory, but few of them are ever likely to see the effect of these efforts. For one thing, children get inspired. Seeing or meeting a player makes a connection that is massive in a youngster's eyes, and it can create a lifelong affinity with the sport.

While few go on to play tennis at the highest level, they are the ones who, as adults, buy the tickets to watch the next generation of players. Consider Andy Roddick. For him, the story of the 2007 Davis Cup by BNP Paribas was a case of coming full circle. As a boy, Roddick looked up to the great American players who defeated Switzerland in that final in Fort Worth: John McEnroe, Jim Courier, Pete Sampras, and Andre Agassi. All those names are important to Davis Cup history, even if Agassi and Sampras sometimes caused more headlines for the ties they opted not to play than for those they did.

Roddick now joins them. He graduated from schoolboy fan to practice partner at the 2000 quarterfinal in Los Angeles, hitting with Sampras and Agassi in the last tie they ever played together. Then, in 2001, Patrick McEnroe blooded Roddick for his second Davis Cup tie against India in post-9/11 America. In 2004, with Roddick as its No. 1, the USA reached its first final for seven years, losing to Spain away in Seville in front of 27,200 spectators. And, in 2007, the team McEnroe had nurtured and Roddick had spearheaded finally won the Davis Cup in the first final played on American soil since that 1992 victory in Fort Worth.

It was a successful graduation for America's top tennis player, and he was the dominant player. Six ties he played, six he won. In fairness, the opposition he faced in 2007 wasn't of the highest caliber—he faced only one player ranked in the top 20—but he carried to the end of 2007 a remarkable record: nine times he had won the decisive point for a USA victory, two of them during his champion year. In a competition that can inspire some to find depths they never knew existed yet cause others to fall apart, that is a truly remarkable achievement.

Roddick was one of several inspirational figures in the 2007 Davis Cup by BNP Paribas. He may have been the player of the year, but his teammates James Blake and Bob and Mike Bryan were all exemplary in their different ways. The Bryans took their Davis Cup record to thirteen wins in fourteen matches and conceded just one set in the four matches they contested during the year. Blake, the man who broke his neck in an on-court accident in 2004—and who had enough sense of the big picture to say it was "the best thing that ever happened to me" because it allowed him to spend time with his father in his last weeks before dying of cancer—published a book detailing his experiences. It ended up on the best-seller list, but of equal importance to Blake was that he ended up with the prize he most wanted in tennis: a Davis Cup winner's medal. In getting there, he triumphed over the doubters who felt he was the weak link

in the American team by posting two vital wins. His victory over Spain's Tommy Robredo in the quarterfinals was crucial because Roddick would not have been able to play on the final day. In the final, he eclipsed Russia's Mikhail Youzhny to give USA a 2–0 lead at the end of the first day that set up a win for USA on the next.

Make no mistake, the Americans won the Davis Cup without an obviously favorable draw. True, they were lucky that an aging Swedish team managed a final fling against the mercurial Argentina, thereby saving the U.S. a trip to the clay of Buenos Aires. But the champions had to exorcise two ghosts: the hold that Gothenburg's almost-mythical Scandinavium arena held over American fortunes, and their "away on clay" jinx in the first round. That was a tough opener, and Roddick hails his victory over Tomas Berdych in the fourth rubber in Ostrava as his most satisfying of the year. Without it, the Davis Cup story could well have been very different.

Among the other heroes of 2007, Igor Andreev, Marat Safin, and Kristof Vliegen all won live fifth rubbers—Andreev twice—and Juan Martin del Potro and Philipp Kohlschreiber posted impressive wins on their Davis Cup debuts.

If proof were needed that the Davis Cup itself is bigger than even the biggest names in the sport, it came at the Switzerland-Spain first round tie in Geneva. World No. 1 Roger Federer declined to play, and world No. 2 Rafael Nadal was unable to play with a late injury, yet the two sides mounted one of the most exciting ties of the year, highlighted by a scintillating doubles before a full stadium.

The defending champions, Russia, looked vulnerable from the first round, but ended up reaching the final thanks to three fifth-rubber wins. Germany had its best year for a decade as Tommy Haas finally came good for his country. And the Davis Cup by BNP Paribas played a part in Serbia's quite sensational year—Jelena Jankovic, Ana Ivanovic, and Novak Djokovic made astonishing progress up the rankings, Ivanovic and Djokovic reaching Grand Slam finals. Djokovic then put the icing on Serbia's cake by taking his still-young nation into the World Group for the first time (as Serbia), at the expense of the twenty-eight-time champions, Australia.

The final may be remembered for being decided inside two days, but it's the first time in ten years that this has happened, and the growing strength in depth in tennis was a factor in a first-round weekend that saw all eight ties still live going into the final day.

And the year had its bizarre element, with rumors circulating for a few days about Tommy Haas having allegedly been poisoned in Russia during September's semifinal. Haas underwent medical tests, but no evidence to support these allegations was unearthed. One day, the story might well form the basis of a gripping fictional detective novel but, in factual terms and as unprosaic as it may sound, Haas merely succumbed to a stomach bug, along with a number of other players, over a dramatic semifinal and play-off weekend.

Ultimately though, the year belonged to Andy Roddick and the United States. And the 2007 Davis Cup stands as a reminder to all athletes of how a performance can inspire the next generation. There may have been another ten-year-old at the final in Portland, Oregon, who was inspired like Roddick was fifteen years earlier. Even if no youngster in Portland ever goes on to represent his country, the USA's win, at the very least, will have created a pool of enthusiastic Davis Cup fans ready to populate stadiums at future ties. And Andy Roddick has bequeathed the legacy he was granted in 1992 to another generation of American fans. ●

Pictured on previous page:
The US and Swiss teams at the 1992 Trophy Presentation
Andy Roddick at 10
Andre Agassi (USA)
Pictured opposite from top:
Mardy Fish and Andy Roddick (USA) at the 2004 Final, won by Spain in Seville
Andy Roddick (USA) played his first live rubber against India in 2001

Pictured from top:
Lleyton Hewitt (AUS), left, and Paul Hanley (AUS);
Chris Guccione (AUS); Belgian celebrations

BELGIUM v AUSTRALIA CONTINUED

singles in the Davis Cup followed a near-identical pattern to his thirty-fifth, in which he had lost the crucial rubber of Australia's 2006 semifinal to Argentina's Jose Acasuso after twice being one set up.

Vliegen, whose game is built around a big serve, had clearly worked out what was going to make Hewitt uncomfortable. Aware that he was up against one of the great counterpunchers, he never gave Hewitt any predictability, mixing up soft shots from the baseline with bouts of explosive winners. "Hewitt had to think that he never could know what I would do," Vliegen said after the match. "He plays the same steady game. If you do what he likes, you will lose for sure."

For a while, the counterpuncher got the better of the exchanges, but Hewitt created eighteen break points, converting just five, and served ten double faults, as Vliegen ran out a 4–6 6–4 3–6 6–3 6–4 winner. To his credit, the Australian refused to use his cold as an excuse for the loss, though the two days' practice it cost him might well have been crucial, given that for the rest of the weekend he was virtually unstoppable. Instead he seized on Vliegen's comments as a source of inspiration, and Hewitt's determination very nearly saw Australia to what would have been only its second-ever comeback from 0–2 down.

As expected, Rochus won the second rubber 3–6 7–5 6–2 6–3, despite conceding thirty-five centimeters (fourteen inches) in a Little v Large contest against the two-meter (six foot, six inches) Guccione. Rochus had beaten the tall left-hander three weeks earlier in a marathon five-setter at the Australian Open. On a surface that showed up Guccione's relative lack of movement, the younger Rochus did so again despite twenty-six aces from the Melburnian.

The doubles was a triumph for Australia, but particularly for Paul Hanley. It took a while for the twenty-nine-year-old to break into the Australian squad, something many connected with Australian tennis thought would never happen, and his unassuming demeanor contrasted dramatically with the fired-up Hewitt. Yet they were the perfect foil for each other in a one-hour-forty-six-minute 6–2 6–4 6–2 demolition of Olivier Rochus and Vliegen. "We gelled well considering that we've hardly played together," said Hewitt. "There were a lot of positives today; it was a pleasure to play with Paul."

When asked about playing Rochus in the first reverse singles, Hewitt made a pointed comment. "We played at Wimbledon last year," he reminded his audience, adding with emphasis "and I won fairly convincingly." It was another case of Hewitt working as hard off-court for his advantage as on it.

When he got on court, the Australian was magnificent. On a surface that makes it very hard to have more winners than unforced errors, his ratio was 56:30—and that after Rochus had staged a remarkable fight back from being just two points from defeat in the third set. Yet Hewitt was not going to be blown off-course, a 6–2 6–3 6–7(4) 3–6 6–1 score seeing him level the tie after nearly eleven hours on court in his three matches.

A year earlier, Guccione had won a live fifth rubber against Switzerland's George Bastl in only his second live Davis Cup singles. That, plus his five-sets win over Max Mirnyi in the 2006 quarterfinals, encouraged Hewitt to say: "Gucc is an underrated player, hopefully he'll go out there and enjoy it." But Guccione didn't enjoy it. Needing a solid serving display to hold his own with a man ranked sixty-six places above him, his serving was only mediocre, and Vliegen took full advantage with a 6–4 6–4 6–4 win. The Belgian never faced a break

point, passed beautifully, and limited Guccione to just ten aces, compared to the thirty-nine the Australian had served in his straight-sets victory over Bastl.

Just as after the Hewitt match, Vliegen was very sanguine about what he had done to take Belgium into its first quarterfinal for eight years. "I didn't have to work for my service games because I was playing aggressively," he said. "Chris was serving well, but I was putting a lot of pressure on his serve, and if you're under pressure for two hours it's normal that you're going to make mistakes. One break per set in three sets—that's what I wanted, and that's what I did."

It made tennis seem such a simple game. And it again emphasized just how hard it is for a team to come back after losing both the opening day's rubbers. ●

AUSTRIA v ARGENTINA

THE DAY HE RETIRES FROM ACTIVE INVOLVEMENT IN TENNIS and whatever else he goes on to achieve, Alberto Mancini should have a monument erected to mark his contribution to Argentinean tennis. His tangible successes as a player, coach, and Davis Cup team captain will no doubt be listed, but perhaps his greatest single achievement was one of changing a mindset.

Until 2005, Argentina was a team that simply didn't travel well. Almost impregnable at home, its players would freeze in various corners of foreign fields. It wasn't just a matter of not being able to play on surfaces other than clay, though Argentina's penchant for clay meant countries hosting the South Americans tended to avoid the red stuff. Argentina didn't play well away. Despite the cosmopolitan nature of the men's tour, the team had a tendency to get unsettled by unfamiliar food, different security procedures, and various other things not to their liking. The result was a poor away record that contrasted sharply with the country's powerful representation in the top 100.

Argentina's visit to Austria in the 2007 first round was just the kind of tie the Argentineans might well have lost before Mancini's reign. Missing their top player, David Nalbandian, they traveled to Linz with a team boasting one complete debutant, one World Group debutant, a player returning from suspension, and a stand-in team leader who had never been comfortable on the fast carpet the Austrians had chosen. It was a recipe for implosion. But Argentina in 2007 was a more robust proposition—a top player's absence was seen as a chance for others to shine, and two men shone brightly as the 2006 runners-up neatly sidestepped the pitfalls fate had set for them.

Linz is best known internationally for its latticed spicy jam cake, the Linzer Torte, reputed to be the oldest cake in the world. It's made with roasted hazelnuts, red currant jam, and spices such as vanilla, cinnamon, and powdered cloves, and looks as attractive as it tastes. The Austrian team that faced Argentina was also looking good: Jurgen Melzer was into the top 30 for the first time, Stefan Koubek had reached the final in Chennai the previous month, and to add extra spice, Austria had a new captain in Gilbert Schaller. Yet it was the visitors who had the icing on the cake, thanks to startling performances from Guillermo Canas and Juan-Martin del Potro.

Pictured from top:

Juan-Martin del Potro (ARG); Sebastian Prieto (ARG), left, and Jose Acasuso (ARG)

AUSTRIA v **ARGENTINA** CONTINUED

Canas had the more emotional story. Suspended in 2005 for a banned diuretic, he had sat out his fifteen-month punishment and returned to the tour in mid-2006, winning five Challenger tournaments in a comeback that showed that the twenty-nine-year-old meant business. There was even talk of him playing in the 2006 final—he traveled to Moscow as his standing with the other Argentinean squad members was very high, but Mancini considered him not ready for the rigors of a final. By February 2007, Canas, by now ranked 107, was the perfect replacement for the exhausted Nalbandian. "This is the restart in my career," Canas said after the draw. "My goal is to break the top 20 but I know it will be a long way. After what happened to me, every time I go on court I'm very happy, and this is Davis Cup so I will most probably be very emotional to represent my country once again."

Any emotions he felt were lightened by the fact that, by the time he took to the court, Argentina was already one up. Jose Acasuso, playing his first match in the Davis Cup by BNP Paribas since losing the decisive fifth rubber of the 2006 final to Marat Safin, beat Stefan Koubek 7-6(6) 6-1 6-4. For a man who doesn't like indoor carpet courts, Acasuso was superb. He never dropped serve, and was particularly solid in the tiebreak, which proved crucial. Koubek had two set points at 6-4 but served a double fault on the second, and was never in it after that. "The double fault was like a knife in my back," the Austrian said.

Enter Canas. Ranked 107 but playing to a level of at least 30, he beat Austria's top player Jurgen Melzer 7-6(6) 6-2 6-4. It was almost identical to the Acasuso-Koubek match— a close first set, decided on an 8-6 tiebreak after Melzer had led 5-3, after which the visiting player opened up and played some highly impressive tennis that clearly took the home nation by surprise. "I'd been looking forward to this match for a long time," Canas said, "and it was very exciting to play like that—it was a great win. I'm happy for myself and I will celebrate, but I'll be happier when the team has won."

Mancini was as near to being ecstatic as such a calm personality will allow himself. "It's a dream Friday," he said. "He [Canas] has been saying he's been playing at a better level than his ranking, and he proved it, but even I was surprised about how well he closed out the match."

By Saturday morning the Austrians were two-down in a tie they had harbored reasonable hopes of winning, and they then lost their new captain. Schaller woke up with the stomach flu, the Austrian team doctor considered it too infectious to have him in close proximity to the players, and his seat was taken by Austria's fourth player, Alexander Peya. But then the home team's fortunes suddenly improved.

With Argentina fielding a first-time Davis Cup pairing of Acasuso and the World Group debutant Sebastian Prieto (Prieto had played one Davis Cup rubber in 1999, an Americas Zone I doubles against Venezuela), the experienced Melzer and Julian Knowle took the doubles 6-3 6-7(2) 6-3 7-5. Prieto was broken in the first and second sets, but became the dominant player as Argentina broke back at 4-5. When the visitors then won the set on the tiebreak, a victory in two days looked plausible, but Acasuso was broken in the first game of the third set, and an inspired game by Knowle at 5-5 in the fourth saw Austria home.

It's part of Mancini's philosophy to hold back a player to be fresh for Sunday's singles, if the strength of his squad allows for it. So when he told the eighteen-year-old del Potro on Saturday night that Acasuso wasn't feeling well, it was a ruse to prepare the exciting Argentinean for his Davis Cup debut. And what a debut it was.

Pictured from top:

Guillermo Canas (ARG); Jurgen Melzer (AUT), left, and Julian Knowle (AUT)

Pictured opposite from top:

Jurgen Melzer (AUT); Argentinean captain Alberto Mancini celebrates with Juan-Martin del Potro (ARG)

It could have been a disaster. Del Potro had to save break points in the opening game, but once he had steadied his nerves, he went on to beat Melzer 7–6(4) 3–6 6–4 4–6 6–2 in three hours and twenty-six minutes. At the end of the second and fourth sets, it seemed the twenty-five-year-old Austrian was set to make use of his greater experience, but del Potro survived a wobbly first game of the decider, played particularly aggressively when returning serve, and broke down in tears after seeing Argentina through.

"It was unbelievable," he said, "this is the best match of my life. The captain wanted to know last night if I felt ready to play, and I said 'yes, I think I can win.' I didn't sleep well at all, but I think that is normal!"

Two comments at the end of the tie testified to the Mancini revolution. Asked how happy he was about winning a five-set debut rubber, del Potro replied: "I'm happy not because I won but because the team won." And Mancini said: "When you play away it's always going to be a tough match, but in the last couple of years we've felt we have a chance no matter where we play." That resilience outside Argentina was to be tested again in the quarterfinals. ●

CZECH REPUBLIC v **USA**

THERE WAS A TIME WHEN ANDY RODDICK would have been in serious trouble for what he did in Ostrava during the USA's tie against the Czech Republic.

The word "serve" in tennis comes from the game's royal roots, when the player of lower social standing began the point and thus "served" the player of higher status (in some cases the king). So when one of Roddick's big serves fizzed into the enclosure occupied by the Czech president Vaclav Klaus, narrowly missing the country's first citizen, the American was perhaps fortunate to be living at a time when he could just put up a hand in apology, without fear of being hauled off to the dungeons and hung upside down from his ankles.

That Roddick should make such an impact with his serve on a clay court was a big part of the USA's success against the Czechs. By the start of 2007, the words "USA—away on clay" had come to instill fear into the hearts of all American tennis fans. It had been ten years since the USA had won a World Group tie on red clay—that was in February 1997, when the Americans fielded the former French Open champion, Jim Courier, against a Brazilian nation boasting a young Gustavo Kuerten still four months away from his shock French Open title. In the intervening years, any team hosting the U.S. chose clay, and the Czech Republic was no exception. The players at its disposal didn't have an especially good record on clay—it was simply that, against an American team boasting two top-tenners and the world's best doubles team, they fancied their chances best on the surface that Roddick (ranked 4) and James Blake (6) had never impressed on.

By winning in the fourth rubber, the Americans lifted the ten-year monkey off their back, but, for no fault of their own, it was a mildly Pyrrhic victory. The Czechs had two top-twenty players in Tomas Berdych and Radek Stepanek, the latter a proven player on

Pictured from top:
Ivo Minar (CZE); James Blake (USA)
Pictured opposite:
Andy Roddick (USA)

the red dirt. Stepanek had sat out the 2006 Davis Cup season, but the appointment of Jaroslav Navratil as the new Czech captain was done with the aim of bringing Stepanek back into the fold. For his own reasons, Stepanek, newly engaged to Martina Hingis, decided to continue his Davis Cup hiatus, and the Czechs' lack of a second player became a crucial factor.

For instead of facing the world No. 19 in a very tricky opening rubber, Roddick faced the world No. 158, Ivo Minar. Admittedly Minar had been preferred to the higher-ranked Lukas Dlouhy (91) for his greater tour experience, but it was still a much more manageable assignment for Roddick than Stepanek would have been. Roddick won 6–4 4–6 6–2 6–3, the five break points he saved in the opening set proving crucial in the outcome of the match, and possibly the weekend.

Despite being ranked 12 compared with Blake's sixth, Berdych leveled the tie with a 6–1 2–6 7–5 7–5 win. Blake admitted that Berdych played "unbelievably well," but it was once again a sign that Blake needs several matches to find his feet on clay and is not the player he normally is when coming straight off another surface. After two quick-fire sets that left the match level after just fifty minutes, Blake double-faulted on set point in the third, and suffered a controversial overrule in the fourth on a point that would have given him a break.

Yet Roddick's win had given the Americans breathing space, and Bob and Mike Bryan were never likely to lose the doubles to Dlouhy and Pavel Vizner. They didn't deliver their best performance, but they still won 6–4 6–4 6–4, breaking Dlouhy in the tenth game of all three sets for what they described as "spooky symmetry." "We raised our level at the right time," said Mike Bryan. "They had more break points than we did, but we won the big points—maybe we were a little lucky today."

For the eighth time, Roddick took to the court on the Sunday of a Davis Cup tie playing for America to win. The previous seven he had won—his only defeats had come with the U.S. 1–2 down. That record looked threatened when Berdych took the first set with a solitary break, but Roddick wasn't worried, and when he broke in the second game of the second set, the tide turned. From then on, Berdych got frustrated, and Roddick ran away with the second and third sets. The fourth was more even, but Berdych netted a forehand at 4–6 in the tiebreak, as Roddick ran out a 4–6 6–3 6–2 7–6(4) winner to seal America's victory.

The Americans' World Group jinx on clay had been broken, and Patrick McEnroe's team was rewarded with a home tie against Spain. ●

BELARUS v **SWEDEN**

WHEN YOU'VE BEEN DRAWN AWAY SIX TIMES IN A ROW, you yearn for a home tie. When another trek comes out of the hat, that's bad enough, but the task facing Sweden in its seventh successive away tie was one of the toughest assignments in the Davis Cup by BNP Paribas in the first decade of the twenty-first century: facing Belarus in Minsk.

Pictured from top:
The U.S. team at the official dinner; Lukas Dlouhy (CZE), left, and Pavel Vizner (CZE)
Pictured opposite from top:
Tomas Berdych (CZE); the U.S. team celebrates

Pictured from top:

Vladimir Voltchkov (BLR); Belarusian cheerleaders;

left to right: Thomas Johansson (SWE), Jonas Bjorkman (SWE)

and Swedish captain Mats Wilander

Pictured opposite from top:

Robin Soderling (SWE); Belarusian captain

Serguei Tarasevitch, left, and Max Mirnyi (BLR)

BELARUS v **SWEDEN** CONTINUED

Belarus was an unlikely tennis power. It only came into being as a sovereign state in 1993, and from the start was governed by a president who had made no secret of his wish to one day reunite his country with Russia. Yet from this nation of precarious statehood emerged two players, Max Mirnyi and Vladimir Voltchkov, who built up an impregnable fortress in their home stadium, the Football Manege in the center of the capital.

So when Sweden had to travel to Minsk in February 2007, did their players groan at the task? Well, no—in fact, almost the opposite. "It's a relief after several ties on clay finally to have one on a quick surface," said Jonas Bjorkman, Sweden's veteran doubles specialist. With Mats Wilander able to name Thomas Johansson to his squad, alongside Sweden's top player, the big-serving Robin Soderling, it seemed a team well equipped for a quick carpet. By the end of the weekend Johansson was saying it was the fastest court he could ever recall playing on, and Wilander offered the assessment: "Belarus at home—that's someone you don't want to play!"

But by then, the Swedes had created their own little piece of history. They had inflicted Belarus's first home defeat in nearly twelve years. It was mighty close, though, and involved one of the Davis Cup's matches of the year.

The Football Manege was only completed in 2003, and its first Davis Cup tie was Belarus's ecstatic fifth-rubber victory over Russia in the 2004 first round. Built in the middle of Minsk as a winter training center for soccer players, it generates superb atmospheres for Davis Cup ties, though some of that is orchestrated. Several dozen young cheerleaders dressed in Santa Claus costumes (yes, in February) and wielding pompoms, underwent a thorough practice session on the Wednesday of the tie, so that when play began on Friday, the support for the home side was a veritable chorus of approval.

In the run-up to the tie, much was made of the fact that Bjorkman and Mirnyi would be up against each other. For the previous three years, the pair had become one of the world's top doubles combinations, and great friends. They arrived in Minsk as the world's second-best partnership behind Bob and Mike Bryan, and were one and two in the individual doubles rankings. After the draw, Mirnyi said: "I'm happy that the day has finally arrived—there has been many months of waiting for this tie and it's a unique one because a big part of the Swedish team are my close friends. So I'm proud to have them come and visit my home town and home country, but we have to put all the private issues aside and be as professional as possible."

There was much speculation about whether Bjorkman would face Mirnyi on the opening day, but Johansson was preferred for the match that looked the pivotal rubber of the weekend, the second of the five.

The tie opened with Soderling's 6–3 7–6(3) 6–1 victory over Voltchkov. Since reaching the Wimbledon semifinals in 2000, Voltchkov's only achievements of note had come in the Davis Cup, a competition that always brought out the best in him. By February 2007 his ranking was down to 730 and there were doubts about his fitness, yet such was his team record that when he invoked an old Russian proverb, "Once a year, even an unloaded gun may shoot," it didn't seem entirely fanciful. And when he had two set points in the tenth game of the second set, he was on the verge of creating serious problems for the world No. 26. But Soderling served too well, and once those two chances had gone, Voltchkov's game fell away badly.

In retrospect, Johansson's 6–4 6–4 6–4 win over Mirnyi was indeed the crucial result of the weekend. Mirnyi has so often come in to level the tie after a Voltchkov defeat, but even at nearly thirty-two, Johansson was a player still capable of Grand Slam–winning quality, and a break toward the end of the first set put him on a course he was never to deviate from.

The 2–0 scoreline seemed to have taken the romance out of the doubles, with Bjorkman expected to ride the wave of Sweden's momentum to seal Sweden's victory. As it happened, Bjorkman delivered one of his least distinguished Davis Cup performances, while Mirnyi was solid and Voltchkov brilliant. Bjorkman lost his serve in the twelfth games of the first and third sets, as Mirnyi and Voltchkov beat him and Simon Aspelin 7–5 4–6 7–5 6–3. Yet Wilander is convinced that the most important statistic in the doubles was the match time. The three hours and twenty-five minutes it lasted proved crucial in the rubber of the weekend.

When Soderling lost the first and third sets on 10–8 tiebreaks against Mirnyi in the first reverse singles, the tie seemed headed for a live fifth, with the chance for the home side to bounce back from the 0–2 opening day deficit. At 6–5 in the fourth, a live fifth rubber was a point away as Mirnyi earned himself two match points. But Soderling saved them both, and then finally won a tiebreak to take the match into a fifth set. The tide had turned, and a break in the sixth game of the decider allowed the Swede to shepherd his country into its first quarterfinal since 2004 with a 6–7(8) 7–5 6–7(8) 7–6(3) 6–3 scoreline that had taken exactly four hours to compile.

Afterward, Mirnyi admitted that the psychological and physical toll of playing his third best-of-five match in three days had become a factor late in the fourth set, but he added: "I'm sure this match will be remembered for a long time." No doubt, but as the fans left the Football Manege, they must have wondered what might have happened if Mirnyi had converted one of his two match points. For while it's unfair to read anything into a dead rubber, Voltchkov did beat Johansson in straight sets, just to add a little extra anguish to only the second home Davis Cup defeat for Belarus in its fourteen years of existence. ●

FRANCE v ROMANIA

OF THE EIGHT FIRST-ROUND TIES, only one looked a foregone conclusion. France's strength in depth and Davis Cup experience seemed no match for a Romanian team heavily reliant on two players, one returning from a long injury layoff, the other thirty-three years old. Ultimately the task did prove too great for the visitors, but the tie in Clermont-Ferrand lasted into the third day, thanks to an exhilarating doubles in which Romania's lesser names proved their country's stars.

By 2007, there was no longer an ITF award for junior doubles team of the year, but the second-last pairing to win the award—in 2002—was Romanians Florin Mergea and Horia Tecau. The contrasting duo featured the height and power of Tecau, allied to the craftsmanship and finesse of Mergea. But when, with France already 2–0 up, they faced Arnaud Clement and Michael Llodra, who had won four of their five Davis Cup doubles, it

Pictured from top:
The stadium in Clermont-Ferrand; the French team;
the doubles rubber
Pictured opposite:
Richard Gasquet (FRA)

Pictured from top:

Horia Tecau (ROU), left, and Florin Mergea (ROU);

Sebastien Grosjean (FRA)

Pictured opposite from top:

French fans; Andrei Pavel (ROU)

FRANCE v ROMANIA CONTINUED

seemed a hopeless cause. Four hours and thirty-five minutes later, it was the Romanians who ended victorious, forcing the French to wait until Sunday afternoon for their moment of triumph.

The French pair understandably tried to overpower the smaller Mergea early on, and the break of Mergea's serve in the sixth game was enough to give the home side the first set. But a break of Clement's serve in the twelfth games of the second and third sets gave Romania a 2–1 lead. When Llodra sealed the fourth-set tiebreak with an ace, he let out a loud cry as France seemed to have the momentum going into the fifth.

The decider lasted seventy-seven minutes, but far from the French taking command, it was the less experienced Romanians who gained in strength. They faced just one break point, and once again pounced on a poor Clement service game, breaking him for 10–9. Tecau held serve to love for a 3–6 7–5 7–5 6–7(3) 11–9 victory.

It was a great triumph for Romania, but in truth, French hopes of a seventh consecutive quarterfinal were never seriously threatened. Richard Gasquet had opened against Victor Hanescu, who was short of match practice and hadn't won a tour-level match for ten months following a serious back injury. Gasquet's previous three Davis Cup singles rubbers had all gone five sets, but this one lasted just ninety-three minutes, the 16th-ranked Frenchman winning 7–5 6–2 6–2.

Sebastien Grosjean's selection for the second singles against the thirty-three-year-old Andrei Pavel ahead of his old friend Clement ran counter to their respective rankings (Clement was at 35, Grosjean 45). But France's captain, Guy Forget, said he felt Grosjean was playing better tennis, and, after a slow start, the player proved his captain right by winning 4–6 5–7 6–3 6–1 6–2. Proving wrong the French newspaper that had said Grosjean was "almost retired," the twenty-eight-year-old notched up his third career victory from two sets down, though without ever coming seriously close to losing. Pavel won five games on the run from 2–5 down in the second set, saving several set points, to open a two-set lead. Yet once Grosjean had broken in the second game of third set, the momentum shifted noticeably, the fourth set lasted just twenty-eight minutes, and a break in the second game of the fifth ended Pavel's resistance.

After winning the doubles, Romania's one hope was that Gasquet might falter, having never previously won two Davis Cup singles in the same weekend. But even the wily Pavel couldn't stem the tide, and Gasquet won 6–3 6–2 7–5. The match had some wonderful backhand exchanges, but only in the third set did Pavel make any impact on the gifted Gasquet—he began chipping his backhand to keep the ball low, and opened up a 5–2 lead. But a superb running forehand pass helped Gasquet break back, and the statistics that showed forty winners for the Frenchman, compared to just thirteen unforced errors, testified to the growing quality of the boy so long touted as the future of French tennis.

It had been a very amicable tie. The only dissonant words came after it had been decided, and they came from Forget's normally diplomatic mouth. He lambasted the world No. 1 Roger Federer for not playing for Switzerland, accusing him of demeaning the Davis Cup. Federer's presence would certainly have enhanced the first round, but the drama and closeness of the eight ties had shown that the competition is bigger than any individual, even arguably the greatest individual ever to have played tennis. ●

43

FLASHBACK

THE CZECH REPUBLIC'S HOME TIE AGAINST THE AMERICANS IN 2007 was the USA's first visit to the Czech Republic since the dramatic quarterfinal of 1996, which proved the early high water mark of the modern Czech tennis nation. And it was a triumphant return for one of the vanquished Americans from eleven years earlier, Patrick McEnroe.

In 1996 the Czechs were in only the fourth year as a nation independent of the Slovaks, with whom they had been compatriots since 1918. Czechoslovakia won the Davis Cup in 1980 and throughout the '80s was a formidable nation, spearheaded by Ivan Lendl but with impressive backup from Miloslav Mecir, Tomas Smid, Milan Srejber, and others. When the Czechs and Slovaks split at the start of 1993, the Czechs retained Czechoslovakia's place in the Davis Cup World Group, but it was only in 1996 that they mounted a serious challenge.

The Americans who traveled to Prague were in various kinds of turmoil. They were the defending champions, thanks to the defining weekend of Pete Sampras's Davis Cup career in the 1995 final in Moscow. But Sampras, somewhat dispirited by how little ice he felt his heroics had cut back home, said he wouldn't play until the semifinals. Andre Agassi and Jim Courier had also declared themselves unavailable, and Michael Chang, who had won his two singles in the USA's victory over Mexico in the first round, declined to travel to Europe for the quarterfinal. Add to that Patrick McEnroe's ailing shoulder that would require surgery three weeks later, and U.S. captain Tom Gullikson's worries over his ailing twin brother, Tim (who passed away the following month), and it was a tough assignment.

Despite the USA's defeat, McEnroe remembers the tie with some positives. "People used to say we were the B-team or even the C-team, but it didn't really worry us, we just got on with it. I remember being struck by how rapidly Prague was changing. I went down to Wenceslas Square and the Charles Bridge, and remember thinking it was a free-for-all for capitalism."

In the Sparta Sports Hall, the Czechs had laid a fast carpet but were nearly undone on the opening day. The weekend was a personal triumph for Todd Martin. So often chastised for his fragile nerve under pressure, Martin won his two singles rubbers in straight sets, dismissing Petr Korda on the first day. Korda, ranked 41, was on his way back from a career-threatening injury but was still a quality player who enjoyed Grand Slam glory less than two years later. There was no glory that day, as Martin dismissed him for the loss of just eleven games.

As his second singles player, Gullikson had picked MaliVai Washington, who had made his Davis Cup debut three years earlier but had never been subsequently recalled. Two months later he reached the Wimbledon final, but in retrospect, his five-set defeat to Daniel Vacek in the second singles was the crucial rubber of the weekend. Had the American won, Czech hopes would have been all but extinguished by bedtime on Friday. As it was, Vacek had given the Czechs a lifeline.

With the home team ditching its nominated pairing of Martin Damm and Jiri Novak in favor of Korda and Vacek, the Americans were suddenly under pressure. McEnroe double-faulted on the opening point of the match, and he and Patrick Galbraith won just eight games in a hugely one-sided match in which Korda was outstanding. With Martin putting in another superb performance in the first reverse singles, Gullikson must have wished he had risked Martin in the doubles with either Galbraith or McEnroe.

Martin's win over Vacek took the tie into a live fifth rubber that pitted Korda against Washington. This was Korda's moment. The man who looked like the human embodiment of the Woodstock character from the Charlie Brown cartoons, and who was renowned in the tennis world for his scissor kick in the moment of victory, thrived on the adrenaline rush that winning the first set tiebreak gave him. From then on, the outcome seemed never in doubt, and with his straight-sets win, the Czechs raced to their first—and so far only—semifinal as an independent sovereign state.

Sampras may have been available for the semifinals, but the USA hadn't qualified for them. Instead the Czechs lost a home tie to Sweden, and they have never been beyond the quarterfinals since. ●

Pictured opposite
from top:
Left to right: U.S. captain
Tom Gullikson,
Patrick Galbraith (USA)
and Patrick McEnroe;
Left to right: Cyril Suk (CZE),
Daniel Vacek (CZE),
Petr Korda (CZE),
Jiri Novak (CZE) and
Martin Damm (CZE)
celebrate victory

CUP CROWDS

More than half a million fans watched Davis Cup by BNP Paribas around the world in 2007.
Passionate crowds help to create the competition's special atmosphere.

quarterfinals 6-8 APRIL

Russia defeated France 3–2   MOSCOW, RUSSIA—INDOOR CLAY

Germany defeated Belgium 3–2   OSTEND, BELGIUM—INDOOR CLAY

USA defeated Spain 4–1   WINSTON-SALEM, NC, USA—INDOOR HARD

Sweden defeated Argentina 4–1   GOTHENBURG, SWEDEN—INDOOR CARPET

Pictured on previous page:

The Davis Cup trophy on display in Moscow

Pictured from top:

Paul-Henri Mathieu (FRA); Mikhail Youzhny (RUS)

Pictured opposite from top:

Marat Safin (RUS); the Russians cheer on their doubles team

QUARTERFINALS

IT WAS OVER THE EASTER WEEKEND that the geography of the 2007 Davis Cup by BNP Paribas shifted dramatically.

Up to then, it had looked like being South America's year. True, Chile had been surprisingly beaten at home in the first round, but Argentina looked set to go all the way. In fact, the Argentineans' biggest obstacle seemed to be their away quarterfinal to Sweden. That looked winnable against a Swedish quartet boasting two thirtysomethings and a debutant, and after that it would probably be home ties in the semis and final.

But Sweden hadn't read the script, and on a weekend that saw just what passion the Davis Cup can arouse—even in that much-maligned team-tennis nation, the USA—the likely destination of the 2007 competition shifted to the northern half of the Americas. ●

RUSSIA v FRANCE

UNLIKE THE EIGHT FIRST-ROUND TIES, all of which were live on the final day, only one of the four quarterfinals was not decided by Saturday night, and it was fitting that it should be the tie touted in advance as the battle of the captains. And what a battle it proved to be.

Having gotten France to punch above its weight when it reached three finals in four years (1999–2002), Guy Forget had seen his team suffer four slightly disappointing years and had come to feel that he needed something new for his *equipe*. He had the burgeoning Richard Gasquet as effectively the team leader, he had a solid doubles team in Arnaud Clement and Michael Llodra, and he had four or five players competing for the second singles slot, headed by Sebastien Grosjean, Paul-Henri Mathieu, Julien Benneteau, Marc Gicquel, and Gilles Simon. But would that be enough to beat Russia, led by the wily Shamil Tarpischev?

Forget had studied the strategies used by the likes of Tarpischev and Argentina's Alberto Mancini, and had noticed a common thread: they tended to leave one quality singles player fresh for Sunday duty. In theory, a top-level player ought to have been able to play a five-set match on Friday, recuperate on Saturday, and return refreshed for Sunday. But Forget had noticed that the fresher players tended to win the decisive matches. He therefore gambled by leaving out Clement and throwing in both Grosjean and Mathieu.

History will record that the gamble failed. It did, in the sense that France lost the tie, and the five-set doubles defeat Grosjean and Llodra suffered can be considered the pivotal rubber. But hindsight can blind one to the realities of the pre-tie period, and in many ways Forget got it absolutely right for the tie in Moscow's Luzhniki indoor arena. The arena was built for the 1980 summer Olympics, and the Moskva River meanders around it like a snake encircling its prey. For all of Forget's tactics, it was the Russian snake that once again wrapped itself around the hapless French.

If there was one rubber France probably reckoned on losing, it was the opening one, in which the world No. 4, Nikolay Davydenko, faced France's honest but inconsistent Davis Cup campaigner, Mathieu. Mathieu had posted some reasonable results on the American hard courts but didn't seem to have enough to hurt the wall-like retrieving and big hitting of Davydenko. And when Davydenko took the first set in just thirty-four minutes, Mathieu

Pictured from top:
Sebastien Grosjean (FRA) is congratulated by his teammates;
Igor Andreev (RUS)

looked almost out of his depth. Around two hundred French fans, self-dubbed the "Moscoutaires" (the English would be "Moscowteers"), were making their presence felt, but there seemed a gulf in class between the two players.

Yet no one can ever bank on Davydenko. Inscrutably brilliant one moment, chaotically erratic the next, he played a bad game at the start of the second set, and the doubts took root. He later said he had played the match like a hard-court contest, not his first official outing of the year on clay. He began to play a bit like a clay-courter midway through the fourth set, but by then the Frenchman had settled into a solid groove, and it was just too solid for the erratic Russian.

It wasn't the first time Mathieu had covered his team in glory. He beat the world No. 6, Carlos Moya, in the opening rubber of the 2004 semifinal, only to see his team's chances wither following a wrist injury suffered by Fabrice Santoro during the second singles. But this time looked to be different. His 2–6 6–2 6–1 7–5 win seemed to be the one the French needed to beat their nemesis, and with Gasquet up against Mikhail Youzhny in the second singles, the visitors looked set for a commanding overnight lead.

Yet history will probably recall that the tie took place at a time when Gasquet was again questioning what it would take for him to make the transition to the very top in tennis. "He's like a Ferrari," said Forget of the twenty-one-year-old he was trying to fashion into a team leader, "there isn't anything that Roger [Federer] can do that Richard can't." Maybe, but the difference is that Federer had long since worked out how to do what he needed to at the right moment, whereas Gasquet had still not put it all together on a consistent basis. Federer had also created that aura of invincibility telling his opponents that if they had a chance against him, it would be just the one, and if they blew it, they would live to regret the missed opportunity. Gasquet, by contrast, gave Youzhny two chances, and the Russian seized the second of them.

Gasquet had looked strangely subdued in the first two sets. He lost his opening two service games to love, but as he got into the match in the third set, Youzhny began to struggle with his movement. When the Russian stumbled in chasing a wide backhand, it looked as if he might have to retire. He played on, but the feeling in the arena was that he would have to win it in the third set if he was to win at all. After two hours and eighteen minutes, Youzhny had two match points at 6–5 15–40. No one knew it at the time, but the match had not even reached the halfway mark.

As it went into fourth and fifth sets, the drop shot that Youzhny had netted on his first match point—with Gasquet stranded at the back of the court—looked likely to prove very costly. The ailing but thoughtful Youzhny was reduced to slicing everything off his backhand wing with no pace. Instead of bringing out the fighting cockerel in Gasquet, it seemed to lull him into a stupor of indecision. In the end, Gasquet was fortunate to see Youzhny play a poor twelfth game, which allowed the Frenchman to level.

Though the cramps had gone, Youzhny looked weak in the fifth. He also looked to have missed his chance when he squandered three break points in the eleventh game. But he broke in the thirteenth and served out the victory, winning 6–2 6–3 6–7(8) 5–7 8–6 in four hours and forty-eight minutes as Gasquet netted a backhand—two and a half hours after Youzhny's first match point.

Forget was unusually despondent that evening. "I really thought Richard was going to get that point," he said, his lips tight with the frustration of seeing his man stage a remarkable fight back but still prove unable to complete the job. At the start of the day the captain would have settled for a 1–1 scoreline, but having had Mathieu upset the odds in the opening rubber, Gasquet's defeat felt like an opportunity missed.

Forget knew his decision to play Grosjean might give him a weaker doubles team. It did, but the damage was done less by Grosjean's lesser doubles pedigree compared with Clement than by a tactical error by the French and a tactical masterstroke by Russia.

Tarpischev had named his two first-round heroes, Marat Safin and Igor Andreev, as his doubles team, but then pulled Safin out in favor of Davydenko. It wasn't a completely bizarre selection—Andreev and Davydenko had played doubles at the 2004 Kremlin Cup and won the title—but they were not natural doubles players. And yet their unorthodoxy in doubles helped them unsettle the only quality doubles player on the court.

The French were still thought to have the advantage because of Llodra's doubles caliber. His accurate left-handed returns land regularly on the opposing service line, forcing the incoming server to volley from below the height of the net. But what happens if the opponent isn't at the net? Both Andreev and Davydenko opted to stay back after every serve. Both Russians' serves were big enough for them to win countless free points, but even when the serve alone didn't do it, the Llodra returns were landing on the service line, allowing the home players to crunch their big groundstrokes and undermine the French crowding of the net. As the match wore on, the Russians became more and more dominant.

The error the French made was not to switch to similar tactics when it became clear that Grosjean's serve-and-volley strategy wasn't working. For a set and a half it worked fine, but Grosjean didn't vary the tactic—somewhat surprisingly for one of the great thinkers of the game—and the Russians gradually got the hang of undermining his serve. It was Grosjean who was broken in the twelfth game of the second set and the eighth of the third, as Russia turned a soporific start into a two-sets-to-one lead. But three successive breaks early in the fourth allowed France back, and after two hours and forty-eight minutes, it was all square.

Neither team had an advantage in the fifth set, but still Grosjean persisted with coming in after every serve. In the eighth game he was punished for it, as Russia broke him for the fourth time, and moments later Andreev served out the 3–6 7–5 6–3 3–6 6–3 victory.

It was time for Forget's tactics to prove themselves. He wanted fresh legs on the final day, so the assumption was that Grosjean would play. But in place of Mathieu or Gasquet? In the end, it was Gasquet who stood aside, claiming not to have recovered fully from his four and three-quarter hours of playing Friday night. Perhaps it was more a mental thing, and maybe Forget would have dropped him anyway, but Grosjean was in and Gasquet was out.

Yet who had taught Forget his tactics? Shamil Tarpischev. And Tarpischev brought in Andreev for his first singles match of the weekend—as he always intended to. Something had to give, and ultimately the all-court guile of Grosjean won out over the brute brawn of Andreev. At times Grosjean looked in danger of being overpowered by Andreev's merciless forehand, but the Frenchman's anticipation and speed around the court meant Andreev could never get comfortable, and with the tie's third successive five-setter, Grosjean leveled the score with a 7–5 4–6 2–6 6–3 6–4 win.

Pictured from top:

Nikolay Davydenko (RUS); Richard Gasquet (FRA)

Pictured from top:
Tommy Robredo (ESP); Andy Roddick (USA)

Pictured opposite:
Bob and Mike Bryan (USA) celebrate with captain Patrick McEnroe

RUSSIA v FRANCE CONTINUED

For the third time in four Russia-France ties, the destiny lay in a live fifth rubber. For Forget there was really no decision to make—it had to be Mathieu (the only alternative was Llodra, who on clay was never a serious option). For Russia—well, what a bunny to be able to pull out of the hat on Easter Sunday! Tarpischev had held Safin back until the fifth rubber and threw him in against Mathieu, who may have lost his previous two live fifth matches against Russia but in the meantime had won a live fifth against Sweden's Thomas Johansson in February 2006.

In the first set, Mathieu looked comfortable, matching Safin's brutally flat groundstrokes. But once Safin had taken the first-set tiebreak, he was away and went on to win 7–6(3) 6–3 6–2. Mathieu was very mature about the fact that his best just wasn't good enough and refused to be drawn into any syndrome-talk about having lost a third decisive fifth rubber against Russia.

And fair enough, because he had come up against that increasingly rare but ever-possible phenomenon of Safin firing on all cylinders. "It was pretty surprising for me that I played such good tennis," the Russian said with a modesty he seemed to be using to conceal the invincibility he had felt on court. "I was injured this week, I couldn't practice, I had blisters on the soles of my feet, so it was pretty amazing that I was able to play such good tennis. I never felt that it was going to five sets, I was pretty confident about that."

Forget had gambled on France having a better chance of winning the final day's singles. The gamble had worked with Grosjean's win, but ultimately Tarpischev had trumped him again with both the doubles display and having two fresh players for the final day. Strategists would have loved it, but in the battle of Forget and Tarpischev, the Russian was winning rather too often for it to be considered a genuine rivalry. ●

USA v SPAIN

WHEN DESCRIBING WHAT IS GREAT ABOUT THE DAVIS CUP BY BNP PARIBAS, players and spectators usually cite the atmosphere the competition generates. Playing for an entity greater than oneself is clearly a major factor, but such atmospheres don't materialize by themselves. They result from a massive amount of organization, much of it in a very short time. That's why the United States Tennis Association, the authorities in Winston-Salem, and the ITF should quietly pat themselves on the back for a quite superb spectacle in which the USA beat Spain.

Like any competition, the Davis Cup has to make sure it is moving adequately with the times while at the same time preserving what makes it so attractive. By and large, the competition is very well accepted, but there is a school of thought that says it still hasn't captured the hearts and minds of the original founder nation, the USA. Those who subscribe to that view should have been in the Lawrence Joel Coliseum in Winston-Salem, North Carolina, over the 2007 Easter weekend.

The USTA has generally chosen arenas with a capacity of around seven thousand in recent years, but this time went for one holding almost 14,500 spectators. The tickets were sold out within hours, and the atmosphere for a tie that was effectively decided

Pictured from top:
Fernando Verdasco (ESP), left, and captain Emilio Sanchez;
James Blake; the Spanish team at the opening ceremony

USA v SPAIN CONTINUED

before the first ball was struck was so electric that the Bryan brothers said it was the best they had played in at any level of tennis. There were indoor fireworks with sparkler fountains, "dry ice" to create a misty effect, a passageway for the players to enter the arena, and other effects such as video screens and state-of-the-art lighting. Rocky Balboa could not have wished for a more glittering entry into a boxing ring.

After his singles, Roddick revealed that the U.S. team had felt the buzz even while standing in the tunnel before the opening ceremony. "I looked at the rest of the guys and said, 'I dare you not to get goose bumps right now.' I think we all failed. It was great."

Had the tie really been as even as it had seemed up to a week before the event, the noise and general support could well have helped the Americans over the finish line. In the end, it may well have carried Roddick's injured hamstring just far enough for victory in a tie that, with hindsight, looks to have been comfortable for the home side but was never far from being precariously in the balance.

The name of the arena was apposite. Lawrence Joel was an American soldier who became a hero in Vietnam in the mid-1960s when he helped more than a dozen wounded U.S. servicemen to safety despite being wounded himself. He was later given the Medal of Honor and had the impressive Coliseum in his home city named after him.

Inevitably, the tie was billed as Roddick v Nadal. The Bryan twins were thought to have the doubles, while the form of James Blake had the home camp a little concerned. So the fourth rubber between the second- and third-best players in the world seemed like it would be the contest of the weekend.

The problem was that both men had leg injuries. Nadal had been complaining for a while of pains in his foot, which his doctor chalked up to playing on hard courts. The Spaniard said he was desperate to play for his country, but having done well at both Indian Wells and Miami, he bowed to medical pressure and withdrew from the quarterfinal a week before.

With their big star gone, Spain was now the underdog, but Roddick had picked up a hamstring injury that had forced him to withdraw from his quarterfinal against Andy Murray in Miami, and he was in a race against time to be fit. Back in 2003, the U.S. captain Patrick McEnroe had taken a lot of persuading to play a specialist doubles team, neither of whom could play singles, and while the Bryans' record in Davis Cup was highly impressive, this was just the situation McEnroe had feared. If he was to pick Roddick, he had to be sure he would survive two singles matches. To keep all options open, Mardy Fish was on standby as a full-fledged practice partner of the U.S. squad.

Ultimately McEnroe opted for Roddick, while Spain's captain, Emilio Sanchez, decided to throw in the left-handed Fernando Verdasco to face the biggest server in tennis. Verdasco had beaten Roddick twice—once on a retirement, the other on clay after Roddick had conceded an ace when match point up—and had taken him to five sets at the 2006 US Open. Playing on a fast indoor hard court in North Carolina was not quite the same as on clay in Rome or even outdoors in New York, but Verdasco knew he could beat Roddick, and that all helped to pile the pressure on Blake in the opening singles against Spain's world No. 7, Tommy Robredo.

It so often happens that the crucial rubber of the weekend is the first one—this was a case in point, and the first set was always likely to set the tone. For nine games there was nothing to separate the two men, their big serves making maximum use of the quick surface. As the set neared its conclusion, the question marks hung over Blake's head. He was emotionally up for the tie, being back in the arena where he had made his Davis Cup debut in 2001, but his form in the previous weeks had let him down in tight situations.

Serving first, Blake had a 5–4 lead as Robredo served to stay in the set. The Spaniard made a couple of errors, Blake upped his level, the crowd played its part, and suddenly a very tight set had gone the American's way. It was the crucial set of the weekend.

Having experienced the ecstasy of winning the Davis Cup in 2004, Robredo wasn't going to let the match go, but from then he looked like a beaten man. By contrast, Blake began to sparkle. He broke early in the second set and was soon two sets up. When the American led 5–1 in the third, it was becoming a procession. But Robredo then began a fight back and narrowed the lead to 5–4. A year earlier, Blake had lost the opening quarterfinal rubber against Fernando Gonzalez from two sets up—was lightning going to strike twice? It wasn't. Blake recognized the danger, held serve to win 6–4 6–3 6–4 in just under two hours, and sealed the first point of the weekend for the hosts.

For a man normally so eloquent, the emotion of Blake's victory had robbed him of fluent speech. "It's tough to express how I feel," he said after the match. "This means so much to me. I have at times been sour after Davis Cup losses, but that's just the highs and lows of Davis Cup. It's so great to win and so tough to lose; this one even more so for me because of the memories of the first time I was here."

The significance for the U.S. lay in the fact that, had Roddick's hamstring flared up again, the team could still have won, with the Bryans favorites for the doubles and Blake quite capable of beating Verdasco, David Ferrer, or Feliciano Lopez in the fifth rubber. It meant both Roddick and McEnroe could relax in the second singles—and the man who paid for that was Verdasco.

Verdasco should have taken the first set. He broke in the fourth game as Roddick started gingerly, and served for it at 5–3. But Roddick broke back, won the first set on a 7–5 tiebreak, and after that was never in danger. Verdasco fought to the end, saving five match points, and given that Roddick pulled out of the following week's tournament in Houston, an event he loves, the hamstring was clearly still an issue. Had Verdasco broken back for 5–5 and claimed the third set, who knows what might have happened. But there is no room for "what if" in sport; Roddick converted his sixth match point for a 7–6(5) 6–1 6–4 victory, and the U.S. was effectively into the semifinals.

With hindsight, Bob and Mike Bryan were always going to beat Spain's Verdasco and Lopez, but in the end it became closer than many people had predicted. After two comfortable sets for the world's best pair, the Spaniards—buoyed by their vital win in the marathon doubles against Switzerland in the first round (see page 19)—struck back in the third set, breaking for 4–2 and sealing Spain's first set of the weekend with a Lopez ace. The fourth went into a tiebreak, and things were getting very nerve-wracking for the home faithful before the Bryans made it eleven wins out of twelve Davis Cup rubbers, thanks to a 7–5 6–3 3–6 7–6(5) scoreline.

By Sunday, the 3–0 scoreline was looking a little less emphatic. Roddick, normally a more-than-willing player of dead rubbers, pulled out of the singles that was originally

Pictured from top:

Feliciano Lopez (ESP), left, and Fernando Verdasco (ESP); the U.S. team fly their flag; the Lawrence Joel Coliseum, Winston-Salem

USA v SPAIN CONTINUED

meant to pit him against Nadal, suggesting his hamstring was still a problem and that the U.S. had had little margin for error. But fate was with the Americans. They had done their preparation, in terms of both the venue and the team, and had not only won but seen their most feared opponent, Argentina, crash out against Sweden. Not that Sweden would be easy for the U.S., but it wouldn't provide an away tie against a clay-court nation, which had been the traditional American Achilles' heel. No wonder Roddick described it as a tie he had enjoyed "as much as any other so far."

As the sun set on the glorious white and pink blossoms of North Carolina's distinctive dogwood trees, things were suddenly looking good for the USA's Davis Cup team. ●

SWEDEN v ARGENTINA

NO ONE SHOULD EVER UNDERESTIMATE SWEDEN, especially in its spiritual Davis Cup home, the Scandinavium in Gothenburg. The golden age of Swedish tennis, which saw the Nordic nation with a population of eight and a half million win the Davis Cup six times between 1984 and 1998, may be over, but in those years Sweden established a reputation that today's inheritors are not willing to relinquish lightly. And Argentina discovered that over a weekend that left the 2006 finalists badly bruised.

Under Alberto Mancini's calm captaincy, Argentina seemed to have banished its vulnerability in away ties. Most of its players would still choose clay, but they had gotten their heads around playing on fast indoor surfaces, and with David Nalbandian returning after missing the first round, the South Americans seemed slight favorites to beat a Swedish team boasting Thomas Johansson ranked 32, Jonas Bjorkman at 35, Robin Soderling the top-ranked singles player at No. 30, and the doubles specialist Robert Lindstedt, who had never played a live Davis Cup rubber.

But under the wily captaincy of Mats Wilander on a very fast court, Sweden proved to be revitalized in 2007, and celebrated by winning on their first visit to the Scandinavium in ten years—indeed their first home tie in four. "The Taraflex surface we chose is faster than anything they play on in tour events these days," explained Wilander. "It's almost like a throwback to a past age. In my time as a player we used to play on surfaces that quick, but today's players don't have much experience on it, and that was the element of surprise we were hoping to catch Argentina with."

The fact that Sweden had won the tie by Saturday evening makes it sound like an emphatic victory. But Wilander said the biggest dilemma he faced was who to play in the doubles. "When you finish the first day 2–0," he said, "the doubles is the easiest of the remaining three rubbers to win. You're still favorites if you lose the doubles, but I knew that our best chance against Argentina was to win on Saturday, which was why it was so important to get the team right."

Logic supports that analysis. Backing Argentina's status as favorites was that Guillermo Canas had come from Miami, where he had not only beaten Roger Federer for the second time in successive tournaments, but had reached the final of the most prestigious of the nine Masters Series events. Yet he came to Gothenburg carrying the wounds of his efforts

Pictured from top:

Argentinean fans; Robin Soderling (SWE);

Thomas Johansson (SWE), left, and captain Mats Wilander

Pictured opposite from top:

Thomas Johansson (SWE); David Nalbandian (ARG)

59

Pictured from top:
Jonas Bjorkman (SWE); Guillermo Canas (ARG), left,
and David Nalbandian (ARG)

on the North American hard courts, and it was little surprise that he was not ready for play on the opening day. That suited Argentina's captain Mancini fine, as it allowed him to keep his trump card for Sunday. But the Swedes ensured that Sunday would be irrelevant.

Argentina had a perfect stand-in for Canas in Juan-Martin del Potro, the 1-metre-96 (6ft 5in) eighteen-year-old who had impressed on his Davis Cup by BNP Paribas debut two months earlier. Assuming Nalbandian would beat Sweden's No. 2 Johansson in the opening singles, del Potro would have been able to go out with all guns blazing and Argentina would have been in a strong position. The script was to be somewhat different.

So often Argentina's talisman, Nalbandian produced one of his least effective weekends in the Davis Cup. After taking a typically Nalbandian-like first set on the tiebreak, he looked set to increase his lead toward the end of the second. But the set went into the tiebreak, and once Johansson had taken an early lead, the Swede rolled back the years to claim the shootout 7–2 and level the match.

Though no one could have known it at the time, that was the crucial moment of the whole weekend. Nalbandian dropped his serve in the opening game of the third set, as Johansson—playing his first home Davis Cup tie for six years—suddenly grew in confidence. The Swede took two breaks in the third set and didn't concede a point in the fourth-set tiebreak as Sweden took the opening rubber 6–7(3) 7–6(2) 6–2 7–6(0). Johansson described it as "the best Davis Cup match I have ever played," and it was probably one of the most important too. (A strange footnote is that all three of the Davis Cup quarterfinals being played in Europe had seen the first rubber decided in four sets after the loser had taken the first and looked by far the stronger player.)

With Argentina one-down, del Potro couldn't be quite so relaxed about the second rubber against Sweden's No. 1, Soderling. Using his power well on the fast surface, the Argentinean held his serve firm until midway through the third set, but by then he had lost two tiebreaks. He led both thanks to early minibreaks but couldn't sustain it, and by 4–3 in the third, Soderling had grooved his returns. Having waited thirty-one games for the first break, three suddenly came in succession, as a 7–6(4) 7–6(4) 6–4 victory saw Sweden to a 2–0 lead.

When asked several weeks later what he would remember most from the weekend, Wilander said: "The agony of having to tell Robert Lindstedt that he wasn't playing doubles. I had led him to believe he would play, I intended him to play; after all I had picked him because we felt we needed a change from Simon Aspelin as the partner for Jonas [Bjorkman], but I woke up on Saturday morning with this conviction that I needed to play Johansson, and telling Robert that an hour before the match was terrible."

It was also an act of faith, for while Johansson is a perfectly sound doubles player, he had lost his previous two Davis Cup matches when partnering Bjorkman. Mancini's decision to abandon Sebastian Prieto for the doubles in favor of the in-form Canas seemed more straightforward—why hold back the big guns when there was no more margin for error?

After a set, Mancini was sitting more confidently on his bench. His team was returning more effectively, and a blistering return by Nalbandian on break point in the tenth game saw the visitors take the first set. But once Sweden had won the second on the tiebreak, Argentina lost heart. It was as if Nalbandian suddenly felt the match was going the same way as his singles, and the Swedes were rampant in the third and fourth sets. Bjorkman returned like he did in his best days, Johansson also grew in confidence, and the Swedes won 4–6 7–6(4) 6–2 6–3.

The Scandinavium was ecstatic. Six of the eleven sets had gone to the tiebreak, and the hosts had won five of them. Sweden was in its first semifinal in six years, and after waiting so long for a home tie, the reward was a second one, with the USA as guests. The choice of venue was easy: the Scandinavium, where the Swedes had beaten the Americans three times. Wilander's wonders were summoning up the power of Sweden's Davis Cup history. ●

BELGIUM v **GERMANY**

THE ONLY DAVIS CUP DEBUTANT among the four World Group quarterfinals was Philipp Kohlschreiber. When he played his first Davis Cup by BNP Paribas rubber in Ostend's Sleuyter Arena, he joined the ranks of those touring professionals who don't quite know what hits them when they play for their country. "I was monster-nervous," the twenty-three-year-old Bavarian said, "there were so many emotions, and the support from our fans was amazing—you don't have that kind of support at a tour event."

The remarkable thing is that Kohlschreiber wasn't talking about playing in one of Germany's magnificent indoor arenas in front of twelve thousand adoring fans, but in front of between one hundred and two hundred in a five-thousand-seater arena away from home. True, Germany shares a border with Belgium, so it wasn't like traveling to California for the several dozen loyal German fans. But it was in the North Sea city of Ostend, about as far from Germany as Belgium can manage. Yet it only takes a couple of hundred vociferous supporters to lead a player into uncharted waters.

That Kohlschreiber embraced the atmosphere and channeled it into one of his best tennis displays goes a long way to explaining why Germany was the first of the quarterfinalists to make it to the last four. Some players are intimidated by the responsibility, others thrive on it, and when two who thrive come together, it makes for a thrilling spectacle. Belgium's Olivier Rochus revels in the Davis Cup atmosphere, but even with his home fans chanting "Oli, Oli," he couldn't counteract an inspired debut by Kohlschreiber.

The German had come into the team on the basis of his clay-court prowess. With Tommy Haas the team's mainstay, and Alexander Waske and Michael Kohlmann the established doubles pairing, the only selection problem for Germany's captain, Patrik Kuhnen, was his second singles player. In the first round, Benjamin Becker had made an assured if ultimately unsuccessful Davis Cup debut, but he was widely acknowledged to be weaker on clay than both Florian Mayer and Kohlschreiber. Though Kuhnen nominated Kohlschreiber, he took Mayer to Ostend as well and only informed them of his decision to pick Kohlschreiber on Tuesday.

After an opening ceremony in which Kohlschreiber admitted to having goose bumps when the German national anthem was played, he had three hours to settle his nerves while Haas opened the tie against Belgium's hero from the first round, Kristof Vliegen. On a slow clay court which—inevitably for a surface laid for just one week—had its fair share of bad bounces, Vliegen picked up where he had left off against Chris Guccione in the first

Philipp Kohlschreiber (GER); Tommy Haas (GER); German supporters

61

round. He took the first set against Haas, and as the second moved toward its sharp end, the home player looked the more secure. But then disaster struck.

At 5–5, Vliegen attacked the net, and Haas threw up a lob that Vliegen tried to smash. The Belgian takes up the story. "I turned my back to the wrong side. Everything in my lower back blocked. My muscles around there were sore. They were cramping faster and faster. The physio did a good job, but after that I was not able to play at a good level. Until then I was playing well but I missed too many volleys after that. My weapons didn't work out."

As Haas waited for the trainer to complete his work, his mind went back to Germany's Play-off Round tie of September 2005 against the Czech Republic. Then he had trailed Tomas Zib 6–7 5–5 but bounced back to win. From the same score, he did the same this time. It would be unfair to claim the injury robbed Vliegen of victory—Haas might have bounced back against a fully fit Belgian—but the contest had diminished, and Haas raced to a 5–1 lead in the third set. Vliegen fought back to make the final score 6–7(4) 7–5 6–4 6–2, but his chances had effectively disappeared in the twist of his back.

All was not lost for the Belgians, who had their No. 1 player, Olivier Rochus, up against Germany's No. 2, Kohlschreiber, the home man taking an advantage of twenty-two ranking places into the match. But Rochus had missed ten days of practice after injuring his foot in Miami, and no one was sure how well he would play. By contrast Kohlschreiber had his adrenaline flowing from the first point and broke the experienced Belgian twice in the first set.

By the time Rochus found his game, he was two-sets down, and his legs were beginning to feel the ten-day absence. He saved a match point at 5–4 in the third set, but fell away from Kohlschreiber at 4–4 in the tiebreak, the German winning 6–3 7–5 7–6(4).

All was effectively lost for Belgium now. The small north-west European nation, which has punched well above its weight in Davis Cup, has always been vulnerable in the doubles, and with Vliegen's back not responding to acupuncture treatment, Belgium's captain, Julien Hoferlin, brought in Christophe Rochus to partner his younger brother. They took the first set against Kohlmann and Waske, but from the moment Christophe lost his serve in the first game of the second set, the German pair capitalized on the fact that they were playing more regularly together on the tour and won the match 4–6 6–2 6–3 6–1.

Germany had reached the semifinals of tennis's top team competition for the first time since 1995. Then, it had all ended in tears, when Russia's Andrei Chesnokov saved nine match points in the fifth rubber in Moscow to beat Michael Stich in five sets. Though the Germans didn't know it at the moment that Kohlmann's ace confirmed their place in the last four, they would be on their way to Moscow again. In 1995, Germany, with Stich and Boris Becker, had been firm favorites against the still-emerging Russians but had lost one of the great Davis Cup ties. This time Germany would send a team of underdogs to challenge the defending champions but would know no fear.

"We have worked so long for this," said Kuhnen, the low-key captain who had done so much to create a team spirit among a group of honest but temperamentally diverse professionals. "I am impressed with the way my team played, and we deserve our place in the semis. But we want more now."

Kuhnen's team was about to get a lot more—and on a much bigger stage than the one on which they had performed in Ostend. ●

Pictured from top:

Kristof Vliegen (BEL); Olivier Rochus (BEL); Germany celebrates its victory

Pictured opposite:

Tommy Haas (GER)

63

FLASHBACK

2002 FINAL: RUSSIA DEFEATS FRANCE 3–2 IN PARIS

THE 2007 RUSSIA-FRANCE QUARTERFINAL was the fourth time the two nations had met in the previous six years, in a series dating back to the most dramatic final in recent times, the 2002 title clash in Paris. That weekend is best remembered as the only time in Davis Cup history that a player came back from two sets down to win the decisive fifth rubber of a final. But it would be unfair to let Mikhail Youzhny's remarkable win against the luckless Paul-Henri Mathieu monopolize the memory of an entire weekend of entertainment and drama.

In the first year of BNP Paribas's sponsorship of the Davis Cup, the final fell appropriately in the bank's home city of Paris, with the French putting down a temporary clay court in the Bercy arena, best known for staging the BNP Paribas Masters.

Russia had never won the Davis Cup. Yevgeny Kafelnikov had steered his still-young nation (in post-USSR terms—Russia played for the first time as an independent country in 1993) to two finals in 1994 and 1995, and sentiment had it that he was worth a Davis Cup winner's medal before he retired. At twenty-eight and with a phenomenal number of singles and doubles matches on his clock, Kafelnikov was on the verge of retirement, but with a second world-class player in Marat Safin to share the load, the final seemed all set to be Kafelnikov's moment.

The French were defending champions, having won on grass in Melbourne a year earlier, but only two members of the French team were certainties: Sebastien Grosjean in singles and Fabrice Santoro for the doubles. France's captain, Guy Forget, opted for an untried doubles partnership of Santoro and Nicolas Escude, and for the third final in four years, left out Arnaud Clement, preferring instead the twenty-year-old Mathieu.

Mathieu put in a highly impressive debut against the superior Safin, and the set he took during the Russian's four-set win might have given him confidence for a potential fifth rubber. But the star of the opening day was Grosjean. After a set and a half of very even tennis against Kafelnikov, he stormed away to take the last nine games, leaving the Russian a somewhat befuddled figure at the end.

The doubles was one of the best in recent years, with the French coming back from losing the third set 7–5 to post the kind of emotional victory that made most people in Paris believe on Saturday night that the cup was staying in France. Escude had a nasty fall early in the match and played the fourth and fifth sets with strapping around his waist. But with Santoro's magic gradually taking over as the match wore on, the mighty Safin and Kafelnikov were humbled.

Safin bounced back from that disappointment to beat Grosjean in straight sets in the fourth rubber. The third set had the best tennis of the weekend, and the 13–11 tiebreak with which Safin won involved him saving four set points with some outstanding shotmaking. To those in the arena, it seemed to set up Kafelnikov's crowning moment in team tennis.

Yet the night before, Russia's captain, Shamil Tarpischev, had sat down with Kafelnikov and decided that, after eight sets from an ailing body, Russia's best chance of winning a live fifth rubber lay not with its mercurial talisman but with the twenty-year-old Youzhny. It was a risky decision, given that Youzhny had played just four live rubbers and lost them all, but not for the first time Tarpischev would make the right call.

After all the drama involving the established names, the 2002 Davis Cup was in the hands of two twenty-year-olds whom few outside tennis had heard of. After a set and a half, Youzhny had his head in a towel with embarrassment and frustration. Mathieu was playing solid tennis and riding the wave of Youzhny's nightmare. For two and a half sets it all went France's way, until suddenly the Russian developed a little consistency. From then on, he undermined Mathieu's fragile confidence little by little, and after surviving a scare toward the end of the fourth set, Youzhny established his piece of history with the clock nearing 10 p.m.

Youzhny had created Kafelnikov's triumph, leaving Mathieu in tears. He had also put a dent in France's confidence against Russia, a dent that had still not been straightened out five years later. ●

Pictured opposite:

Mikhail Youzhny (RUS) shows

off the Davis Cup trophy

PRIDE OF A NATION

In Davis Cup, players wear their countries on their sleeves—and their backs, and their kit—and fly their flag at home or away.

semifinals 21–23 SEPTEMBER

Russia defeated Germany 3–2 MOSCOW, RUSSIA—INDOOR CLAY

USA defeated Sweden 4-1 GOTHENBERG, SWEDEN—INDOOR CARPET

SEMIFINALS

THERE WAS A DISTINCT sense of ghosts that needed to be exorcised hanging over the semifinals weekend.

Celebrating being in the last four for the first time in twelve years, Germany was confronted with a visit to the scene of its previous semifinal: Russia's Olympic Stadium, and another makeshift clay court to bring the memories of the dramatic and controversial 1995 clash flooding back (see page 80). But this time the balance of power had shifted—if in 1995 the Germans were strong favorites fielding Boris Becker and Michael Stich against an emerging Russian nation, the German lineup of 2007 was much less experienced than the cup holders, who seemed to have in their pool of players the right man for every occasion.

The USA's ghost in Sweden was Gothenburg's Scandinavium arena, scene of three previous visits and three previous defeats for reasons not entirely connected with pure tennis. The mythical stadium seemed to be Sweden's main weapon in a tie that appeared strongly to favor the Americans.

And wreaking additional havoc was a bug that seemed to be spreading alarmingly around the entire global tennis circuit. It was the joker that played a part not just in the two semifinals but in the play-off ties as well. ●

RUSSIA v GERMANY

TIES IN MOSCOW PITTING RUSSIA AGAINST GERMANY should come with a health warning. If recent experience is anything to go by, they are a danger to players' fitness, spectators' heart rates, and even clothing and court surfaces. A mixture of illness, injury, and even soul-searching struck the 2007 Russia-Germany semifinal in Moscow, yet the various afflictions turned it from an unpromising prospect into one of the ties of the year, full of good tennis and immense human drama.

It peaked in the doubles, where the Davis Cup by BNP Paribas's ability to bring a supreme effort out of a player was once again illustrated in grand style. Russia's Dmitry Tursunov and Mikhail Youzhny were up against a scratch German pairing of Alexander Waske and a man who had never played in the Davis Cup before, Philipp Petzschner. The visitors were impressive in the opening set, and when they won the third set on a 7–4 tiebreak to take a 2–1 lead, it was hotting up nicely. But then disaster struck for the Germans.

"We were up 2–1 in the fourth set and getting very excited," recalled Waske, "when suddenly I heard this clicking in my right elbow. I felt like I can't hit another ball. I thought the match was over, which was very sad because we were the better doubles team. Our physio tried everything to release the pressure on whatever is broken here, I don't know what it is. Tons of painkillers in me."

A subsequent examination revealed Waske had ruptured not just a muscle in his elbow but a group of muscles, a very serious injury that would keep him off the tour for several weeks. Although he didn't know that at the time, he told Petzschner he thought he might not be able to finish the match. "Don't tell me that," retorted the Davis Cup debutant. "We just have to get the ball back and be like a wall."

Pictured on previous page:

The Olympic Stadium, Moscow

Pictured from top:

Alexander Waske (GER), left, and Philipp Petzschner (GER);

Philipp Kohlschreiber (GER)

So Waske continued playing. When it came to his serve he was almost plopping the ball over—"it was a little girl's serve" was how he described it. But does that mean it was easy to play against? Not at all. Ask Ivan Lendl, who lost one of the most dramatic matches in tennis history at the 1989 French Open because his ailing opponent Michael Chang gave him no pace. It was a similar situation here—Petzschner serving at full pace, Waske just pushing the ball over the net. And it worked—Youzhny and Tursunov were thrown, their returning unable to cash in on Waske's extreme pain.

Somehow the Germans forced the fourth set into the tiebreak. This was their one and only chance. Lose it and Waske would have had to quit. Win it and Germany would go into the final day with an unlikely 2–1 lead. Erecting a wall at the net with their reflex volleys, the German pair proved impregnable, winning the tiebreak 7–5 and going into raptures on sealing a 6–3 3–6 7–6(4) 7–5(5) victory. If Waske was the brave warrior defying the pain, Petzschner was the inspiration, seizing the day to take on the dominant role. "It was a ridiculous effort from the newcomer," Waske said of his partner.

And yet, and yet. From the moment the quarterfinal results set up this tie, it was hard to see how Germany could get to three points on a clay surface that did nothing for its top player, Tommy Haas. And so it proved. In retrospect, the sheer fact that it took Russia a live fifth rubber to win is great testimony to Germany's emergence as a genuine Davis Cup team, but even with a 2–1 lead on Saturday night, it was hard to see how the depleted visitors could claim one of the two reverse singles, and for the fourth tie running, Russia won on a live fifth rubber.

In fact, it was an uphill battle for Germany from well before the team set off for Moscow. First they lost their doubles stalwart, Michael Kohlmann, to a knee injury during the US Open. That meant that the German doubles team that had been one of the discoveries of the previous three ties was not an option. Then their luggage was seized by Russian customs, and the squad was forced to attend the formal official dinner on the Wednesday night wearing tracksuits and jeans. Germany's captain, Patrik Kuhnen, apologized for the casual attire but explained it was not the players' fault. And then as the tie got going, Germany's two ever-presents of the previous four ties, Haas and Waske, were struck down, Waske by that elbow injury, Haas by a viral infection.

Not that Russia was spared the gust of the ill wind. Already without Marat Safin, who had gone mountain climbing in the Himalayas—to "find his soul" as Haas described it— they found Nikolay Davydenko ailing after his opening singles. Yet such carnage creates room for heroes to emerge, and emerge they did. Ironically, Germany can claim three heroes from the weekend—Waske, Petzschner, and Philipp Kohlschreiber—while Russia can claim only one, Igor Andreev. Yet it was Andreev who walked off with the fifth point, to break German hearts on the Sunday night, just as Andrei Chesnokov had done in the exact same arena twelve years earlier.

The Davis Cup format of each nation's top player facing the opposing No. 2 on the first day is designed to elicit 1–1 scorelines and thus guarantee the tie will be live on the Sunday. So when Andreev, Russia's No. 2, crushed the eleventh-ranked Haas 6–2 6–2 6–2 in the opening rubber in just over two hours, the tie looked lost for Germany by mid-afternoon Friday. But for all his consistency on the tour, Davydenko had become an

Pictured from top:

Tommy Haas (GER); Nikolay Davydenko (RUS);

Dmitry Tursunov (RUS), left, and Mikhail Youzhny (RUS)

increasing liability in the Davis Cup, and in the second singles against Kohlschreiber, he faced the kind of steady and unflappable opponent who knew how to stick around and exploit the flaws that gradually emerged in Davydenko's game.

Kohlschreiber's 6–7(5) 6–2 6–2 4–6 7–5 win was the single most impressive performance of the weekend. The German soaked up Davydenko's blistering start, knew which shots to play that would feed his opponent's growing anxiety, and held his nerve when Davydenko first won the fourth set and then opened up a 4–2 lead in the fifth. "This is one of my best matches," said the understated Bavarian after his four hours and twenty-three minutes of hard labor. "It's a great feeling that you only have in the Davis Cup. It's unbelievable and I am just happy now." Davydenko blamed experimentation with string tension to reduce the burden on an elbow niggle for his inconsistency, but for the second tie running, he had been found wanting with only a week to change surfaces, and his decision to play the tournament in Beijing the previous week cannot have impressed his captain, Shamil Tarpischev.

If Kohlschreiber was Germany's hero on Friday, Waske and Petzschner were the heroes on Saturday, though few people were around to see it. The Olympic Stadium was sold out, but there were masses of empty seats. Perhaps the Russian tennis public expected little of the doubles; or perhaps they knew that, with the 1–1 Friday scoreline, all the vital action would take place on Sunday. There was also a high-level sports conference taking place in Sochi on the Saturday, which may have sucked some people away from Moscow. But by Sunday, they were all back, a full house in situ to see another Russian fightback.

With Haas too weak to play a best-of-five-sets rubber, Petzschner was given his chance in singles following his superb showing in the doubles. But if he had had little time for nerves a day earlier while playing alongside a teammate, in singles the enormity of the situation struck home for the twenty-three-year-old from the opera metropolis of Bayreuth. His nerves were to be the leitmotif against Youzhny, a replacement for Davydenko who was reported to be under the weather, as the Russian found the right notes. Petzschner was paralyzed. "My arm wouldn't work and my feet wouldn't move," he said after his 6–4 6–4 3–6 6–3 defeat.

"Yesterday I was pumped and having fun so I didn't have any thoughts, but today I felt what it means to play Davis Cup," Petzschner added. "I felt some pressure and I think I was putting the pressure on myself to reach the final. I was saying I have a good chance to win if I play like yesterday. I told myself to stay like yesterday, calm down, relax, take it easy, have fun, go out there, but I couldn't do it."

That left the destiny of the tie with the two heroes from the opening day, Andreev and Kohlschreiber. With his big forehand, Andreev was always going to be the aggressor, and having won two previous live fifth rubbers he was also the favorite. But Kohlschreiber answered Andreev's first set by taking the second.

Kohlschreiber looked tired in the third as Andreev's forehand ripped the German's defenses to shreds, but Kohlschreiber held his own in the fourth. A break in the eighth game allowed Andreev to serve for the match, but Kohlschreiber recovered from 40–0 down to save three match points. On Andreev's fourth, the Russian went for a crosscourt backhand and mishit it, but it landed beyond Kohlschreiber's reach, and the Russians were into their fifth Davis Cup final.

Pictured from top:
Philipp Petzschner (GER); Mikhail Youzhny (RUS);
the Russians congratulate Igor Andreev (RUS)
Pictured opposite:
Philipp Kohlschreiber (GER)

And among the crowd there to enjoy the 6–3 3–6 6–0 6–3 triumph was Safin. He had apparently arrived at the base camp of the world's sixth-highest peak, the 8,200-meter Cho Oyu he had intended to climb, but had decided that maybe he needed a little more conditioning before attempting to find his soul at such heights. Given that the surface in the Olympic Stadium had been put down for him, it was perhaps fitting that he was at least there to witness the victory, if not on this occasion to create it. ●

SWEDEN v USA

TO MANY PEOPLE, Sweden's bequest to the world amounts to self-assembly furniture, Bjorn Borg, and the iconic pop group Abba. And there's a line in "Waterloo," the song that launched Abba in 1974, that goes: "The history book on the shelf is always repeating itself." That was very much a factor in the Swedes' decision to host their Davis Cup by BNP Paribas semifinal in Gothenburg; in fact, the biggest obstacle for the USA in the tie against an aging Swedish side was the ghost of the Scandinavium.

The venerable arena in the center of Sweden's second city did its best to thwart the American tennis fraternity once more, but its powers of influence seemed to be sapped by an outstanding display in the doubles by the Bryan brothers. By Sunday afternoon, its empty rows of seats testified to the hall having given up the fight, and the USA's moment of triumph took place in near silence.

Gothenburg's indoor arena, normally used for ice hockey, has an almost mythical place in tennis folklore. In 1984, with Sweden having earned home rights for the forthcoming Davis Cup final against the Americans, the Swedish tennis association broke new ground by building a makeshift indoor clay court. It had never been done on that scale before—when Sweden beat Czechoslovakia to reach the final, it was clear that clay would be the Swedes' best surface to face the U.S., but no outdoor venue in Sweden in early December was possible, so clay was out. Only it wasn't, and the idea of temporary clay courts for Davis Cup ties was born.

The final was massively hyped. The Americans brought their strongest-ever team—in ranking terms—to Gothenburg: the world's two best players John McEnroe and Jimmy Connors, and McEnroe and Peter Fleming were the No. 1 doubles team and unbeaten in Davis Cup. It was all set to be a massive spectacle. And it was—but for all the wrong reasons. Connors, never a good team player, freaked out at handling immense pressure in a team environment, and his behavior in the opening rubber against Mats Wilander was probably the worst of his career (it included him shaking the umpire's chair with rage, and he came within one warning of disqualification in an era of more lenient standards for behavior than today's). McEnroe was somewhat fazed in his singles, losing to Henrik Sundstrom, and when McEnroe and Fleming "choked"—by their own admission—in the doubles, the Swedes were winners within two days.

Twice in the 1990s, an American team returned to the Scandinavium. On both occasions there were no questions about their behavior, but both times Pete Sampras was struck down by an injury that clearly helped Sweden to victory. So when Sweden chose

Pictured from top:
James Blake (USA); the Swedish team; Joachim Johansson (SWE)
Pictured opposite:
Igor Andreev (RUS)

the Scandinavium for the 2007 semifinal, in which it could parade no player ranked in the top 50 against two top-tenners and the world's best doubles team, it seemed the ghost of the Scandinavium needed to play a part.

It looked like it would do so on the Friday morning. All four American players woke up with flulike symptoms. Nothing was said publicly—in fact, the U.S. Tennis Association's exercise in keeping the information quiet was largely successful—but the handful of people watching Bob and Mike Bryan practicing on Friday morning could have been forgiven for wondering if these were two players preparing for a singles.

The previous day, talk had been rife about the USA's record in Gothenburg. "I don't think it will play much of a part," said Sweden's captain, Mats Wilander, adding scurrilously, "Of course it always helps that we have never lost to the U.S. team in this stadium, but it's a new tie every time. I think everyone in Sweden who follows Davis Cup knows that Sweden has beaten the U.S. three times here." His opposite number, Patrick McEnroe, had said: "We feel this is a new team and a new time. We would love to get a win here for the U.S. Davis Cup and for history, but we don't care much about what happened ten or twenty years ago." Yet surely he must have wondered on the Friday morning whether Gothenburg had a hypnotic hold on the health of American tennis players.

Set against that background, the American victory was a triumph for the team ethic and sense of positive thinking that McEnroe had nurtured in his seven years as captain. It was also a moment of greatness for Bob and Mike Bryan, who provided the only lasting memories of quality tennis from a weekend that ultimately failed to live up to its promise.

Roddick came out against Sweden's unknown quantity Joachim Johansson and played a very tight match to win 7–6(4) 7–6(3) 6–3. In fairness, Johansson was playing his first match for eight months after a second round of shoulder surgery, but he looked sharp, served beautifully, and had put some extra pep into his crosscourt backhand. Roddick needed to be close to his peak to dismiss the Swede's spirited challenge.

Blake was clearly more flat than he was admitting in the second singles, but he was up against an opponent whose ranking of 56 and age of thirty-two were highly misleading. Thomas Johansson had won five of his nine titles on low-bouncing indoor carpet courts and had admitted earlier in the week that the court Sweden had chosen for the tie was better suited to his game than to any of the other seven nominated players. He proved it in a 6–4 6–2 3–6 6–3 victory that briefly threatened to get interesting when Blake took the third set, but the Swede never seemed to have lost control.

That set the scene for the best match of the weekend by far. The Bryans were bringing to the match a Davis Cup record of eleven wins in twelve matches, but Mike Bryan had said after the draw that this would be their toughest match in the competition. They were up against Jonas Bjorkman, a legend in doubles and at age thirty-five still ranked 11th, and Simon Aspelin, a thirty-three-year-old who had just won his first Grand Slam title partnering the Austrian Julian Knowle in the US Open doubles. It may well have been the Bryans' toughest assignment in tennis terms, but they rose to the occasion magnificently.

The first set was outstanding. The Bryans had five break points in the seventh game and were first ahead in the tiebreak. But once the Swedes had got back the minibreak, the tension, drama, and quality of tennis all rose. Both sides had three set points each.

Pictured from top:

U.S. captain Patrick McEnroe; Simon Aspelin (SWE), left, and Jonas Bjorkman (SWE); Swedish fans

Pictured opposite from top:

Thomas Johansson (SWE); Bob and Mike Bryan (USA) with captain Patrick McEnroe

Pictured from top:

Andy Roddick (USA); Jonas Bjorkman (SWE); USA celebrates victory

Pictured opposite:

Andy Roddick (USA)

SWEDEN v **USA** CONTINUED

Bjorkman must have thought he had won the set with a return to Mike Bryan's feet, but somehow the right-handed twin not only got the ball back but steered it down the line for a staggering winner.

By 11–11, all six set points had been saved thanks to first serves. So when Aspelin missed his first serve at 11–12, Mike Bryan stepped in for the second serve. He drilled the ball at Aspelin's feet, the Swede could do nothing with his volley, and fifty-nine minutes of top-notch doubles had ended in the Bryans taking the set.

It was perhaps inevitable that the Swedes should have lost a little heart, but few pairs—either in 2007 or in the history of tennis—could have stayed with the twins in the second and third sets. They were brilliant—bold, brutal, and beautiful to watch. The only blemish was the double fault that gave the Swedes a break-back point at 2–4 in the third set, and Bjorkman was distinctly unlucky to see his return of serve called out when it had clearly beaten the in-rushing Mike Bryan. But this was a day on which the Swedes were the high-quality foils against whom the masters showed their very best, and the numerical record of the USA's 7–6(11) 6–2 6–3 win seems inadequate as a description of their brilliance.

The performance was even gilded by two moments of generous sportsmanship by Bob Bryan. The first came at 2–1 in the tiebreak. Bjorkman volleyed the ball at the lefthander, who appeared to get it back with a reflex volley. His brother Mike rejoiced at the minibreak, and the score was called as 3–1, but Bob admitted the shot had come off his arm, not his racket. Then in the seventh game of the second set, the lefthander got back six defensive volleys and then watched as Bjorkman rifled a forehand long. But as the umpire called the score for the Americans, the taller Bryan admitted the ball had brushed his shoulder, and again the point went to Sweden. It was class, in both performance and ethical terms.

That took the life out of Sweden. On Saturday night there was still anticipation about Roddick's singles against Thomas Johansson. Could the wily carpet court specialist get enough returns back to trouble the fastest server in the game? We will never know, because Johansson woke up with a tummy bug and had to be replaced by Bjorkman. The veteran rallied gamely, but Roddick served too well, especially on his second serves, and was never broken in the two-hour match. As Bjorkman stretched in vain for a backhand volley on match point, Roddick fell to his knees in triumph. "It's what you practice for," he said, anticipating his second final. "It's what you work for. I'm so proud to be part of this team, I'm so proud of my teammates, I wouldn't trade this team for any in the world. I love these guys, and we get another shot at winning the Davis Cup, so I'm really happy right now."

As it happens, the USA won with something to spare. If Bjorkman had beaten Roddick, no doubt Joachim Johansson would have played the fifth rubber, but he was still sore after his exertions against Roddick, and Aspelin, a man with no singles experience at tour level, played the dead rubber.

When Roddick guaranteed the USA's place in the final, it was not clear whom the Americans would face, nor whether they would be at home or away. At that moment, Andreev and Kohlschreiber had split sets in the fifth rubber in Moscow, and a German win would have involved the U.S. traveling to Germany for the final. By the time Blake came off after beating Aspelin, it was clear the Americans would be hosting a Davis Cup final for the first time in fifteen years. ●

FLASHBACK

IN SEPTEMBER 1995 A TWELVE-YEAR-OLD MOSCOW TENNIS FAN CALLED IGOR ANDREEV sat in the Olympic Stadium, watching in ever-increasing awe as Russia's first modern tennis hero, Andrei Chesnokov, pulled off the most unlikely victory against Michael Stich to see Russia through to its second Davis Cup final. It was to be an inspiring moment for the youngster, and for the whole of Russian tennis.

That 1995 semifinal had everything—including controversy on the opening day. Despite having been runner-up to Sweden the previous year, Russia was the underdog, for it faced the ultimate German lineup. Three times the Germans had won the cup, but never with both Boris Becker and Michael Stich on the same team. In 1995 they were together, and not even the choice of clay (Becker never won a tour-level tournament on clay) could dampen the sense that Germany was the strong favorite.

Yet when the two teams arrived in the Olympic Stadium on the Friday morning, they found that the makeshift clay court had been massively overwatered. It made the court, which had already raised some eyebrows as a result of an unusually high number of bad bounces, incredibly slow.

Not that the Germans were worried at the end of a first day that had seen their men play outstanding tennis. Becker had beaten Chesnokov in four tight sets, and Stich had been outstanding in his four-sets win over Yevgeny Kafelnikov, then the world No. 6, which had seemed to end the Russians' hopes.

With Becker and Stich a top-quality doubles team—they not only boasted an impressive Davis Cup record but were 1992 Olympic doubles gold medalists—the Russian pair of Kafelnikov and Andrei Olhovskiy were fighting a seemingly lost cause. The home team won the first two sets, but once Becker and Stich got going in the third and took the tie to a fifth set, it looked like it would be a German victory inside two days. Yet the German recovery faltered at the finish, as Russia took the doubles 7–5 in the fifth.

Still the Germans seemed to be favorites, but the momentum swung back to Russia on Sunday morning, when Becker woke up with his back in severe pain. He blamed the overwatered court for it and ceded his place in the fourth rubber to Bernd Karbacher. Karbacher was no mug—he was enjoying his best year and was ranked 31—but he was not in the same class as Becker and Stich, nor as Kafelnikov, who beat him in straight sets to take the tie into a fifth rubber.

Chesnokov struck first, but when Stich took the second and third sets each 6–1, he looked like the stronger player. Chesnokov bounced back to take the fourth, but Stich again looked to be the more likely winner in the fifth. When the German broke for 7–6, he was serving for a dramatic victory. Nine times he reached match point; nine times Chesnokov saved the day, twice on Stich double faults.

As the tension mounted, Chesnokov twice reached match point at 8–7, but Stich saved them both. Then at 13–12 Chesnokov had two more match points—Stich saved the first but couldn't save the second as the Russian sent Moscow wild. Stich wept into his towel after the four-hour, eighteen-minute defeat, as the likes of Becker and his captain, Nikki Pilic, tried in vain to console him. By contrast, Chesnokov was hailed as a sporting hero and awarded the Order of Courage by Russia's President and number-one tennis fan, Boris Yeltsin.

As for that twelve-year-old boy watching courtside, twelve years later he was himself to beat Germany in a live fifth rubber in the Olympic Stadium to see Russia through to the 2007 Davis Cup by BNP Paribas final. ●

Pictured opposite:

Andrei Chesnokov (RUS)

sends Russia to the 1995 final

TRIUMPH AND DISASTER

A Davis Cup competitor experiences both these things, and plenty more in between.

His response to such emotional highs and lows can shape his entire career.

play-off round 21–23 SEPTEMBER

Serbia defeated Australia 4–1   BELGRADE, SERBIA—INDOOR CLAY

Austria defeated Brazil 4–1   INNSBRUCK, AUSTRIA—INDOOR CARPET

Peru defeated Belarus 4–1   LIMA, PERU—OUTDOOR CLAY

Israel defeated Chile 3–2   RAMAT HASHARON, ISRAEL—OUTDOOR HARD

Great Britain defeated Croatia 4–1   LONDON, GREAT BRITAIN—OUTDOOR GRASS

Czech Republic defeated Switzerland 3–2   PRAGUE, CZECH REPUBLIC—INDOOR CARPET

Romania defeated Japan 3–2   OSAKA, JAPAN—INDOOR CARPET

Republic of Korea defeated Slovak Republic 3–2   BRATISLAVA, SLOVAK REPUBLIC—INDOOR CLAY

BNP PARIB

The bank for a changing

PLAY-OFF ROUND

IN THE FIRST FEW YEARS OF THE TWENTY-FIRST CENTURY, there was relatively little movement between the Davis Cup by BNP Paribas World Group and the top regional zones. Each year, a couple of teams came up and a couple went down, but it was generally limited to two or three changes (in 2003 it was four, but that seemed a real exception). In 2007 six of the sixteen World Group nations lost their places in a weekend of dramatic action that featured everyone in the top 30 who was eligible and nominated to play. And among the casualties were the two nations that had contested the Davis Cup final just twenty-two months earlier. ●

CZECH REPUBLIC v SWITZERLAND

TO THOSE OUTSIDE PRAGUE, the clash between the Czechs and the Swiss will no doubt be seen as the tie that defined the limits of Roger Federer's influence. But to those who were there, two far more positive features stand out in a contest that may have been a play-off tie but would have been a worthy final.

The first was the stadium. The Sazka Arena was built for ice hockey and opened in 2004 as the new permanent home of the Slavia Prague club. Over the play-off weekend it made its debut as a tennis arena, hosting 14,500 spectators who contributed to a tremendous atmosphere. Those who were there say it was indoor tennis at its best.

The second was the breathtaking quality of tennis offered by Federer and Tomas Berdych in the fourth rubber. Federer won the match in three sets, but the level of play was magical throughout. Even the Swiss players, used to sitting on the bench while the maestro struts his stuff, were left with mouths gaping as Berdych matched the level of tennis offered by Federer, forcing the world No. 1 to even greater heights. The match will long live in the memories of those in Prague that day.

Yet by the time Federer sealed his 7–6(5) 7–6(10) 6–3 win, the damage had been done to Swiss hopes. While Stanislas Wawrinka battled bravely against Radek Stepanek, the doubles had left the Czechs in the driver's seat of a thriller that saw Federer and Yves Allegro miss a match point in the third set.

The Czech captain, Jaro Navratil, had thrown caution to the wind by dispensing with his nominated pair of doubles specialists, Martin Damm and Lukas Dlouhy, and replacing them with his two singles players, Berdych and Stepanek. With the Swiss standing at match point in the third-set tiebreak, the gamble looked to have failed. But Berdych saved it with an unreturnable serve, and when the Czechs won the tiebreak 9–7, the momentum began to turn.

A break at the start of the fourth set gave the home side the advantage, and the Swiss missed several opportunities to break back. In the fifth, with the Czechs increasingly successful in playing to the weaker Allegro, they broke in the seventh game. That was enough to see them to a remarkable 3–6 5–7 7–6(7) 6–4 6–4 win.

Pictured on previous page:
Novak Djokovic (SRB)
Pictured from top:
Stanislas Wawrinka (SUI); Tomas Berdych (CZE), left, and Radek Stepanek (CZE);
Roger Federer (SUI)
Pictured opposite from top:
The Czech team celebrates with Radek Stepanek (CZE);
Yves Allegro (SUI), left, and Roger Federer (SUI)

That took the destiny of the tie out of Federer's hands, but with Wawrinka ranked just ten places below Stepanek at 44, the live fifth rubber was no formality. Stepanek inspires mixed emotions on the tennis circuit—he's not the most popular guy in the player lounges, but he has an economical and fluid playing style that can be beautiful to watch. And for his live firth rubber against Wawrinka, he donned a tennis shirt that mirrored the Czech flag, just to let the home faithful know that his two-year absence from the Davis Cup had not dimmed his patriotism.

When Wawrinka had a set point in the twelfth game, the Swiss were still confident. But once he had lost the tiebreak to go one set down, his belief began to ebb away. And Stepanek, having known that the doubles was the crucial rubber, was not going to let his nation's opportunity pass. He had a scare midway through the third set, when he began cramping badly and needed a three-minute timeout to have his leg massaged, but he held on to take the set into the tiebreak. And when a Wawrinka return went wide, Stepanek's 7–6(3) 6–3 7–6(4) victory had not only proved a fitting christening for tennis in the Sazka, but had also sent the Swiss down to Europe/Africa Zone Group I. ●

JAPAN v **ROMANIA**

THE OTHER PLAY-OFF TIE TO GO TO A LIVE FIFTH RUBBER—and to feature one of the rubbers of the year—was in Osaka. Andrei Pavel and Takao Suzuki may not be the most heralded players on the tennis circuit, but those in the Namihaya Dome arena who saw their scintillating five-setter in the first of Sunday's singles will be talking about it for as long as they're talking about tennis.

That Suzuki is likely to end his career without ever playing in the Davis Cup by BNP Paribas World Group is one of the minor tragedies of the competition. A stocky 1.75-meter (5 foot, 9 inch) serve-volleyer, he constantly has a smile on his face and plays the game with an ebullience that suggests it would be a crime not to enjoy it. Whether facing Roger Federer at the Australian Open or a little-known journeyman on the challenger circuit, he is always value for money, and he won all four tiebreaks he played against Pavel and Victor Hanescu—but still ended up on the losing side.

Even at age thirty-three, Pavel was still able to deliver Davis Cup performances of high quality. He had leveled the tie on the opening day by beating Japan's top-ranked player, Go Soeda, but he went into his match against Suzuki with his team 2–1 down. Suzuki had beaten Victor Hanescu in straight sets in the opening rubber, and Romania's doubles heroes from the first round tie against France, Florin Mergea and Horia Tecau, were eclipsed by Suzuki and the lefthander Satoshi Iwabuchi in their match. So the pressure was on Pavel.

It was a match rich in quality and entertaining tennis. Suzuki gave it everything, at one stage ending up tangled in the net after chasing down a seemingly hopeless Pavel drop shot. Pavel helped him to his feet, one of several examples of the great spirit in which the match was played.

When Suzuki took a two-set lead, Japan was just one set away from a place in the World Group, something it had not had since 1985. Yet in his third rubber of the weekend,

Pictured from top:
Andrei Pavel (ROU); Takao Suzuki (JPN)
Pictured opposite from top:
Satoshi Iwabuchi (JPN), left, and Takao Suzuki (JPN);
Victor Hanescu (ROU)

Pictured from top:
Kyu-Tae Im (KOR); Kyu-Tae Im (KOR), left, and Hyung-Taik Lee (KOR) fly their flag;
Lukas Lacko (SVK)
Pictured opposite:
Hyung-Taik Lee (KOR)

JAPAN v **ROMANIA** CONTINUED

the thirty-one-year-old's energy was nearing its end, and when Pavel strolled through the third set to win it 6–1, the tide began to turn.

By then Suzuki was running on empty, and despite the final score of 6–7(6) 6–7(1) 6–1 6–4 6–4, he never came close to victory after the second set. Pavel ran out the winner to level the tie, and Hanescu then beat Soeda in four sets to end a magical weekend in favor of the visitors.

It would be churlish to suggest that Romania's players of the 1990s and 2000s were in the same class as the team of the 1960s and 70s led by Ion Tiriac and Ilie Nastase—after all, Tiriac and Nastase took Romania to the final in 1972, whereas the 2007 tie in Japan was Romania's eleventh play-off round in twelve years. But all four Romanians once again showed that they provided a formidable lineup, and ensured that the modern golden era of Romanian tennis would enjoy at least one more year in the top flight. ●

SLOVAK REPUBLIC v **REPUBLIC OF KOREA**

FOR FIFTEEN YEARS, HYUNG-TAIK LEE TOILED THE PROFESSIONAL TENNIS CIRCUIT as a lone representative of South Korea. He had one notable success in Sydney in 2003, when he beat the then world No. 1 Lleyton Hewitt for his only tour title. There were other triumphs, like a doubles title and a raft of medals of differing metals at the quadrennial Asian Games. Like a good wine, Lee improved with age, to the point where he posted his equal-best Grand Slam result at thirty-one, reaching the fourth round of the 2007 US Open. Three weeks later, he achieved another milestone, taking his country into the World Group of the Davis Cup by BNP Paribas.

It would be no exaggeration to say that Lee did the job singlehandedly. True, he needed a competent doubles partner, and Kyu-Tae Im did the job nicely. But Lee played ten sets in Korea's away play-off tie against the Slovak Republic, winning nine of them, and a thrilling backhand down the line took his country back to the World Group for the first time since 1987.

"I'm very happy," said Lee, who played the tie at a career-high ranking of 39. "This is the fulfillment of a life-long dream for me."

In fairness, Lee stood head and shoulders above the other seven players nominated for the tie. The result might have been different had Dominik Hrbaty been fit—he underwent surgery on a longstanding elbow problem after losing to Lee at the US Open—but his presence as an onlooker only at this tie thrust the Slovak Republic into a rebuilding phase far removed from the glory days of just two years earlier.

Much of global sport goes in cycles, but those cycles have come thick and fast in the Slovak Republic in recent years. It was only in 2003 that the new national tennis center in Bratislava, of which the 4,000-seat Sibamac Arena is the centerpiece, was opened, and by December 2005 it was hosting a Davis Cup final. Yet the 2005 Slovak team of Hrbaty, Karol Kucera, Karol Beck, and Michal Mertinak was in tatters by 2007, with only Mertinak

Pictured from top:
Tim Henman (GBR) with his daughter Rosie; Jamie Murray (GBR),
left, and Andy Murray (GBR); Marin Cilic (CRO)

SLOVAK REPUBLIC v **REPUBLIC OF KOREA** CONTINUED

remaining. And even he had the remnants of a worrying knee injury during the play-off
tie against Korea.

Set against that background, the fact that two teenagers—eighteen-year-old Martin
Klizan and nineteen-year-old Lukas Lacko—were blooded for their first live Davis Cup
rubbers was a good investment for the country's future, even if the Slovaks were always
likely to lose their World Group status. Lacko posted a win, beating Korea's second player,
Woong-Sun Jun, in the second rubber, and Klizan, the 2006 Roland Garros junior
champion, picked up experience in his singles against Lee that could prove useful.

But once the doubles had gone to the visitors, Lee and Im beating Lacko and
Mertinak for the loss of just five games, only illness or injury could have prevented Korea
from advancing to the 2008 World Group. Lacko took the third set off Lee in the deciding
rubber, but it was merely delaying the inevitable.

The Slovak captain, Miloslav Mecir, had always been realistic about his team's
chances, and the 2005 final must have seemed an age ago. But Klizan's debut was a
building block for the future, and with Beck nearing the end of his suspension for taking
a banned substance, the future was not entirely bleak for the Slovaks.

As for the Koreans, they desperately wanted a home tie in the 2008 first round to
boost the profile of tennis back home. They didn't get it—an away trip to Germany
proving scant reward for Lee's superiority on the temporary clay of Bratislava. ●

GREAT BRITAIN v CROATIA

THERE WILL BE SOME WHO SAY that a team so dependent on two players is always
going to come unstuck at some stage, and that Croatia's demise in the 2007 play-off
round was only a matter of time. But seldom can any nation have had such a streak
of bad luck in the run-up to a tie.

The cold Mario Ancic caught in the week of February's first round tie against Germany
proved to be a symptom of a more serious illness, the strength-sapping mononucleosis
virus that kept him off the tour for much of the year. He was back in action by the time
the play-off weekend came around, but a shoulder injury meant he couldn't take his
place against Great Britain on Wimbledon's No. 1 Court (the Centre Court was not up for
discussion as a new roof was being fitted).

If this was the moment for Ivo Karlovic to shine, he declined to take it. The giant Croat
cited "differences with his national association" as his reason for being unavailable, forcing
the association to sound out Goran Ivanizevic on a possible one-off return to the competition
he was so dedicated to during his playing days. Although a regular on the seniors' tour,
Ivanizevic said no, leaving Croatia heavily reliant on Ivan Ljubicic, who was contesting what
he claimed would be his final Davis Cup by BNP Paribas tie. Ljubicic would again need to
play on all three days, with the promising eighteen-year-old Marin Cilic as second singles
player, and the doubles specialist Lovro Zovko partnering Ljubicic on the Saturday.

At least that was what the Croats intended. The loss of Ancic and Karlovic had turned
the tie from a likely Croatia victory to a 50:50 encounter. When Ljubicic woke up on the

morning of the singles with a painful urinary tract infection, the British were suddenly favorites. Cilic, thrust into the role of team leader, showed his potential in taking Andy Murray to five sets, but Roko Karanusic was no match for Tim Henman, the veteran Brit in his final weekend of action who had expected to be facing Ljubicic, and Henman's 6–4 6–3 6–3 victory meant the home nation ended the first day two-up.

When the British captain, John Lloyd, then dropped Andy Murray from the doubles, bringing in Henman to partner Jamie Murray, it seemed like a sentimental decision to allow Henman to end his career with a live win. It was more calculating than that, Lloyd deciding that if the doubles were lost, he would rather have a fresh Andy Murray for the fourth rubber. But the sentimentality worked, Henman striking the winning crosscourt forehand winner as the British took the doubles 4–6 6–4 7–6(3) 7–5 to take a 3–0 lead. Henman took the applause with his eldest daughter Rosie on court with him.

Asked whether it was tough to retire when his country had just returned to the World Group, Henman said: "Not very tough at all. I know the timing is absolutely right for me. I've had a fantastic career, I've had some great moments and it's time to move on, but to be retiring at thirty-three with a family, I definitely appreciate how fortunate I am. And to finish it the way I did today, I couldn't have scripted it better."

The year 2007 will go down as a valedictory one in British tennis. The two standard-bearers of a generation, Greg Rusedski and Henman, retired, and both went out in victorious Davis Cup ties (Rusedski against the Netherlands in the tie that set up Henman's finale against Croatia). The golden duo of British tennis had handed the baton to the next generation by leaving Great Britain in the World Group—but dangerously dependent on just one player, Andy Murray. ●

SERBIA v AUSTRALIA

IF IT WAS GOODBYE TO THE TWO EMERGING EASTERN EUROPEAN NATIONS that contested the 2005 final, it was hello to another emerging nation from that increasingly fertile area of the globe for top-quality tennis players: Serbia. And the way the Serbs qualified for the 2008 World Group was a veritable festival of patriotism cloaked in tennis apparel.

The atmosphere in the Beogradska Arena in the capital, Belgrade, was the kind that all sporting events dream of. Just less than twenty thousand passionate, cheering spectators packed into the arena, making constant noise and whipping themselves into a frenzy for the national cause. The text of Serbia's new national anthem ("new" since the country split from Montenegro just over a year earlier) was printed and put on every seat in the house. When the Serbian players came onto court, the lights were dimmed and they were welcomed to the triumphant strains of Orff's "O Fortuna" from Carmina Burana—by contrast, the Australian players were serenaded onto court with music by AC/DC. It was almost as if tennis was just the vehicle to worship and express love for Mother Serbia.

Inevitably, such passion risked becoming over-nationalistic. Those who witnessed the way Yugoslavia disintegrated in the early 1990s might have found the home support a

Pictured from top:

Lleyton Hewitt (AUS); Nenad Zimonjic (SRB), left, and Novak Djokovic (SRB)

Pictured from top:

Australian captain John Fitzgerald, left, and Chris Guccione (AUS);

the Beogradska Arena, Belgrade; Janko Tipsarevic (SRB)

SERBIA v AUSTRALIA CONTINUED

little excessive, and there was a fine line between the kind of cheerful patriotism that enhances the best of top-level sport and the kind of blinkered nationalism that can lead to ugly scenes. Certainly the crowd was made up largely of fans not accustomed to tennis, and that nearly led to the Davis Cup's "partisan crowd" rule being invoked. Serbia's captain, Bogdan Obradovic, was frequently warned that if his country's supporters didn't calm down a little, they risked Serbia being deducted a point or more. Fortunately it never came to this, but perhaps that was partly because the tie was never allowed to become truly close.

Both sides were heavily dependent on one man. For Serbia it was Novak Djokovic, the rising star of 2007 who by September was third in the world behind Roger Federer and Rafael Nadal. For Australia it was Lleyton Hewitt, still just in the top 20 but not the man he was four years earlier when Australia won its twenty-eighth Davis Cup, and lacking the back-up he enjoyed back then. Both were expected to play on all three days, both aided by a quality doubles player in Nenad Zimonjic for Serbia and Australia's Paul Hanley. It all pointed to a clash of the titans in the fourth rubber between Djokovic and Hewitt.

Everything on the opening day went according to plan. Djokovic entered to a regal welcome to beat Peter Luczak in straight sets. That seemed to set up Janko Tipsarevic for a historic win over Lleyton Hewitt. Once the leading hope of Serbian tennis, Tipsarevic found himself eclipsed by Djokovic, Jelena Jankovic, and Ana Ivanovic in 2007, so a match against Hewitt in his home city was his chance to emerge from the shadows of his more illustrious compatriots. When he led by two sets to one, a great victory was in the cards. But it's a brave person who bets against Hewitt over five sets in the Davis Cup by BNP Paribas, and the Australian was relentless in winning the fourth and fifth sets, both 6–1.

With Hewitt having played five sets, there seemed to be more pressure on Australia in the doubles. Hewitt and Hanley got off to the better start, breaking in the fourth game and taking the first set as the Serbs showed a distinct lack of coordination. The Aussies had a break early in the second, but once that was lost and Hanley was broken at 4–5 for the Serbs to level, the momentum changed dramatically. As the Serb supporters had more to cheer, umpire Enric Molina became as active with his calls for quiet as he was in calling the score. Though no one could have known it at the time, the third and fourth sets saw Hewitt getting weaker, a process that would continue through the night, rendering him unfit for action the following day. Serbia took the doubles, leaving the destiny of the home nation still in Djokovic's hands.

The fourth rubber should have been the culmination of Serbia's joy. To an extent it was, but that joy was muted by Hewitt's absence, the Australian said to be so afflicted by a viral infection that he could barely get out of bed. His place was taken by Chris Guccione, whose massive left-handed serve kept the sets close, but on the big points he was always likely to be second best to Djokovic on clay, and the Serb ran out a 6–3 7–6(3) 7–6(5) winner.

It was Serbia's first passage to the World Group as Serbia—Yugoslavia had been a semifinalist in 1992, and Serbia had inherited Yugoslavia's records in the competition—but there was no place for small details in the euphoria of victory. Serbia had entered the elite of another sport, and national pride was limitless in Belgrade that Sunday afternoon. "This is our territory, here nobody can beat us," said Djokovic, clad in the Serbian flag, to the crowd. Perhaps an international diplomat might have chosen his words more sensitively, but there were few who would have begrudged the home nation their sporting pride that weekend. ●

ISRAEL v CHILE

THE TIMETABLE OF THE DAVIS CUP BY BNP PARIBAS is fairly strict. Matches are played on a Friday, Saturday, and Sunday, and it's normally only rain that pushes a tie into a Monday. But the timing of the 2007 play-off weekend clashed with the Jewish festival of Yom Kippur, and with Israel at home to Chile, the ITF gave the Israeli national association special dispensation to play the tie on Thursday, Friday, and Sunday in the Canada Stadium of Ramat Hasharon. Even then, a marathon, nail-biting final set in the doubles almost forced a clash between tennis and the religious holiday.

The theme of Yom Kippur is atonement for past sins. In tennis terms, Israel's players had no sins to atone for at the end of a pulsating tie that saw eighteen hours and thirty-two minutes of play in the four live rubbers. Israel returned to the World Group for the first time in fourteen years, and that without a player ranked in the top 100. Chile's players also came away from the tie with great credit, both for their role in a superb weekend and also for the dignified way they acknowledged Israel's moment of triumph. In fact, the only atonement was done by one of Fernando Gonzalez's rackets, which he smashed during the dramatic fourth rubber. When asked about it later, the Chilean said only: "It deserved it."

The split in the opening day's singles was good news for Israel. Gonzalez—fresh from winning the title in Beijing a few days earlier that had gotten the best year of his career back on track—beat Noam Okun in four sets as expected, but the win by Israel's No. 1, Dudi Sela, over Nicolas Massu in the opening rubber was crucial for home hopes. On a hard court very similar to the one on which Massu had won the Olympic gold medal three years earlier, Sela beat his higher-ranked opponent in four sets in a staggering five hours and seven minutes—if it had gone to a fifth, the Davis Cup record books might have had to be rewritten.

The eight hours on the opening day worked to Israel's advantage, as they paraded a specialist doubles team in Jonathan Erlich and Andy Ram, going for a seventh successive win in the Davis Cup, against Chile's singles players Gonzalez and Massu. It proved to be the highlight of the weekend in tennis terms.

The absence of a tiebreak in the final set turned the decider into a war of attrition. It also became a battle against time, with the religious festival due to begin at four in the afternoon. Finally, with the clock at nine minutes to four, Massu was broken in the eighteenth game, and the Israelis went into the rest day 2–1 up after an exhilarating 2–6 7–6(1) 6–2 3–6 10–8 victory.

Pictured from top:
Fernando Gonzalez (CHI); left to right: Andy Ram (ISR), Jonathan Erlich (ISR), Fernando Gonzalez (CHI) and Nicolas Massu (CHI); Dudi Sela (ISR)

Pictured from top:

Andy Ram (ISR), left, and Jonathan Erlich (ISR);

Dudi Sela (ISR) and teammates savor victory

Pictured opposite from top:

Max Mirnyi (BLR), left, and Vladimir Voltchkov (BLR); Luis Horna (PER)

ISRAEL v CHILE CONTINUED

Strictly speaking, Yom Kippur is a day of fasting, but there was no way Sela could have fasted before coming out to play the fourth rubber against Gonzalez. For five hours the world No. 105 battled against the Australian Open runner-up, twice coming back from a set down and standing just two points from defeat on four occasions. But once Sela had won the fourth set on a 9–7 tiebreak, he gained strength, broke Gonzalez in the fifth game of the decider, and won on his first match point to send the stadium wild with delight.

"This is definitely the happiest day of my life," he said. "We made an amazing achievement, for tennis in Israel and for all the nation. I just want to get some rest now, I can't breathe."

Gonzalez was magnanimous in defeat: "I was sure that we would win this one, but I have to give respect to the Israeli team that made a terrific job and left me dumbfounded. Sela is a great player and it's a real mystery that he is 105 in the world ranking. He should be top 50."

Sela took a step toward the top 50 by reaching the quarterfinals in Tokyo one week later, a run that allowed him to break into the top 100. And Israel's joy was further enhanced when the draw for 2008 produced a home first round tie just a weekend after Israel's women were due to face Russia, the holders of the Fed Cup by BNP Paribas, also on Israeli soil. Such constellations of lucky breaks can do wonders for the development of tennis.

As for Chile, the three years of hope that had followed Gonzalez and Massu's heroics at the Athens Olympics had ended with a sad exit from the World Group, the period having produced just one World Group win before relegation back to Americas Zone Group I. The Israeli fan who held up a banner in the stadium reading "Welcome to IsraHell" had encapsulated Chile's fate perfectly. ●

PERU v BELARUS

IN 1989 A NINE-YEAR-OLD BOY with dreams of becoming a professional tennis player was among the crowd at Lima's Jockey Club for Peru's first play-off tie. The visitors were Australia, and in Jaime Yzaga, Peru had a player in the top 30 for the first time. Yzaga won both his singles, including a 9–7 fifth-set win over Jason Stoltenberg in the fourth rubber, but Peru's dreams of reaching the World Group were shattered in the fifth, when Wally Masur beat Pablo Arraya in four sets.

That boy was Luis Horna, and eighteen years later, he was determined to shepherd Peru into the Davis Cup by BNP Paribas World Group for the first time. "This is a historic moment for us," he said, "we have been doing this for the last years, same group, same team, same captain—we are ready for this moment."

And yet, as the light started to fade at the end of an absorbing first day at the Rinconada Country Club in Peru's capital, things did not look good for the home nation. Vladimir Voltchkov was doing what he does best—making a mockery of his tour form. The 463rd-ranked player was leading Horna 6–3 7–6(4) 4–2, looking well set to erase the shock defeat of his teammate Max Mirnyi to Peru's No. 2, Ivan Miranda, from earlier in the day. But then Horna won four games on the run, and they proved the key to the entire weekend.

ALL PART OF THE SHOW

Davis Cup ties aren't just three days of tennis. There are also the draw ceremonies, on court presentations, official dinners and press conferences, all integral to a nation versus nation event.

the final
30 NOVEMBER - 2 DECEMBER

USA defeated Russia 4-1   PORTLAND OREGON, USA — INDOOR HARD

Pictured on previous page:

The Americans show off their replicas

Pictured from top:

Andy Roddick (USA)

Dmitry Tursunov (RUS)

THE 2007 DAVIS CUP FINAL CREATED AN OPPORTUNITY BEYOND THE ACTUAL TENNIS. While Dwight Davis's trophy had become so popular around the world that 136 nations took part in the competition, it sadly had lost some of its luster in the nation where it all started. Having the final on U.S. soil for the first time in fifteen years offered the perfect forum to reacquaint the American sporting public with one of its most valuable legacies and with one of the sport's most compelling properties.

Never in the 107 years of the competition had the Davis Cup been out of American hands for more than eleven years. That gap was lengthened to twelve in 2007 but also stopped at twelve as the cup returned home for the first time since Pete Sampras gave his all in the 1995 final in Moscow. The names of New York and Chicago were bandied about as initial favorites to host the final, but ultimately the United States Tennis Association settled on the Memorial Coliseum in Portland, in the West Coast state of Oregon. It proved a fitting venue for a final played with great spirit that attracted a capacity twelve thousand crowd daily, even for Sunday's two dead rubbers. But it also showed how much catching up the Davis Cup needed to do in the United States.

Despite being the competition's founding nation, the USA has a sporting culture that doesn't sit easily with the Davis Cup format. Team sports in the U.S. are based on fixed seasons in the annual calendar, seasons that overlap but generally don't conflict. A competition that takes place over four weeks a year—and not consecutive weeks either but spread over a crowded tour calendar—is foreign and confusing to the American sporting psyche. The continent's biggest sports, American football, basketball, and baseball, feel no need to engage with the rest of the world on any regular basis. In fact, a comparison of one of the USA's most lucrative sporting leagues, the NFL, to international football shows that it is small in global reach compared with soccer's FIFA World Cup. But this is of minor consequence to the American public, so little wonder that the loudest calls for changes to the Davis Cup by BNP Paribas format come from the Americans.

The decision to opt for Portland was partly motivated to create the best possible atmosphere for the final. "When we have taken Davis Cup ties to huge cities like the New Yorks and the LAs," said the USTA's president, Jane Brown Grimes, "it sometimes doesn't get the same support as we've gotten here in Portland. We've found coming to cities of this size is very good for the competition, because the town really embraces it and it becomes a very big event."

There's no question that Portland embraced the Davis Cup community, and the city whose suburb of Beaverton plays host to the headquarters of the biggest sportswear company in the world (Nike) clearly enhanced its reputation as a venue for international sporting events with a near-faultless staging of the final. In fact, the biggest criticism of the host city centered on a week of near-continuous rain, something the locals can hardly be blamed for.

The magnitude of the task facing those trying to take the Davis Cup beyond the confines of the genuinely enthusiastic American tennis public was evidenced via a number of subtle indicators. The morning after the U.S. team had lifted the trophy, half the front page of the local daily newspaper The Oregonian was given over to a sporting story: a college football game known affectionately as "the Civil War" in which Oregon

State University beat the University of Oregon 38–31. Even on the front page of the paper's sports section, the Davis Cup was only the third story. The final was frequently referred to in various media as "the Davis Cup finals" as most American sporting events have a series of finals rather than just one. And much media reporting of the final was done with the tone that a curious circus had come to town, rather than a recognition that the USA was staging one of the year's top events in world sport.

Credit then to The Oregonian's Ryan White, who managed to put the event in some global context. Under the headline "Davis Cup is larger than American life," White wrote of the draw at Portland's Newmark Theatre: "It felt like an event of global interest, which we know is a troublesome concept for an American sports fan. Believe it or not, in a lot of somewheres, the Davis Cup is way bigger than the Civil War." That such a thing needs to be said will horrify die-hard Davis Cup fans, but communication involves speaking the language of the person being communicated with, and the 2007 Davis Cup by BNP Paribas final was a big learning curve for many keen American sports fans.

A marketing executive would say that, set against this background, the optimum scenario would be for a home win in the fifth set of the fifth rubber, generating a spectacle that has people glued to their televisions and wanting more. It didn't quite happen like that; in fact, as a contest the final was killed off on the first day. But sometimes the worthiest champions are worthy because they snuff out all opposition and, with the Russians missing Marat Safin more than they admitted, the USA sailed away with the title.

Safin had declared an end to a troublesome year several weeks earlier. He decided that a body creaking under the wear and tear of ten years on the professional circuit needed a decent break if he was to get any more mileage out of it. At the time he withdrew, it didn't seem a big loss to the defending champions. They had five natural players—one was always going to miss out—and Safin's move meant the decision was taken out of Shamil Tarpischev's hands. But, even with his inconsistency, Safin offered versatility and Tarpischev missed that in Portland.

Perhaps the captain was also misled by Igor Andreev's great prowess on clay. For the opening day's singles, Tarpischev opted for Dmitry Tursunov and Mikhail Youzhny over Andreev and Nikolay Davydenko. Despite being ranked fourth in the world, Davydenko seemed to have lost some of his Davis Cup appetite, especially in singles, and having lost to Andy Roddick in the Tennis Masters Cup in Shanghai two weeks earlier, his omission hardly seemed a surprise. Nor did Tursunov's nomination ahead of Andreev. But after Tursunov's paralyzed display against Roddick in the opening rubber, Andreev would have been a better option, even off his favorite clay. Wonderful thing, hindsight.

It's likely, however, that no Russian could have lived with Roddick on that last day of November, for this was a man with a mission.

Roddick had been taken to the last final on American soil, the 1992 USA–Switzerland tie in Fort Worth, Texas, as a ten-year-old and had been infected by the Davis Cup bug. "It wasn't just the quality of the players," he recalls of the U.S. team that was made up of John McEnroe, Jim Courier, Andre Agassi, and Pete Sampras, "but the fact that I didn't know tennis could be that way, with people going crazy, with the patriotism, with the

Pictured from top:

Igor Andreev and Teimuraz Gabashvili (RUS)

American fans in Portland

Nikolay and Irina Davydenko (RUS)

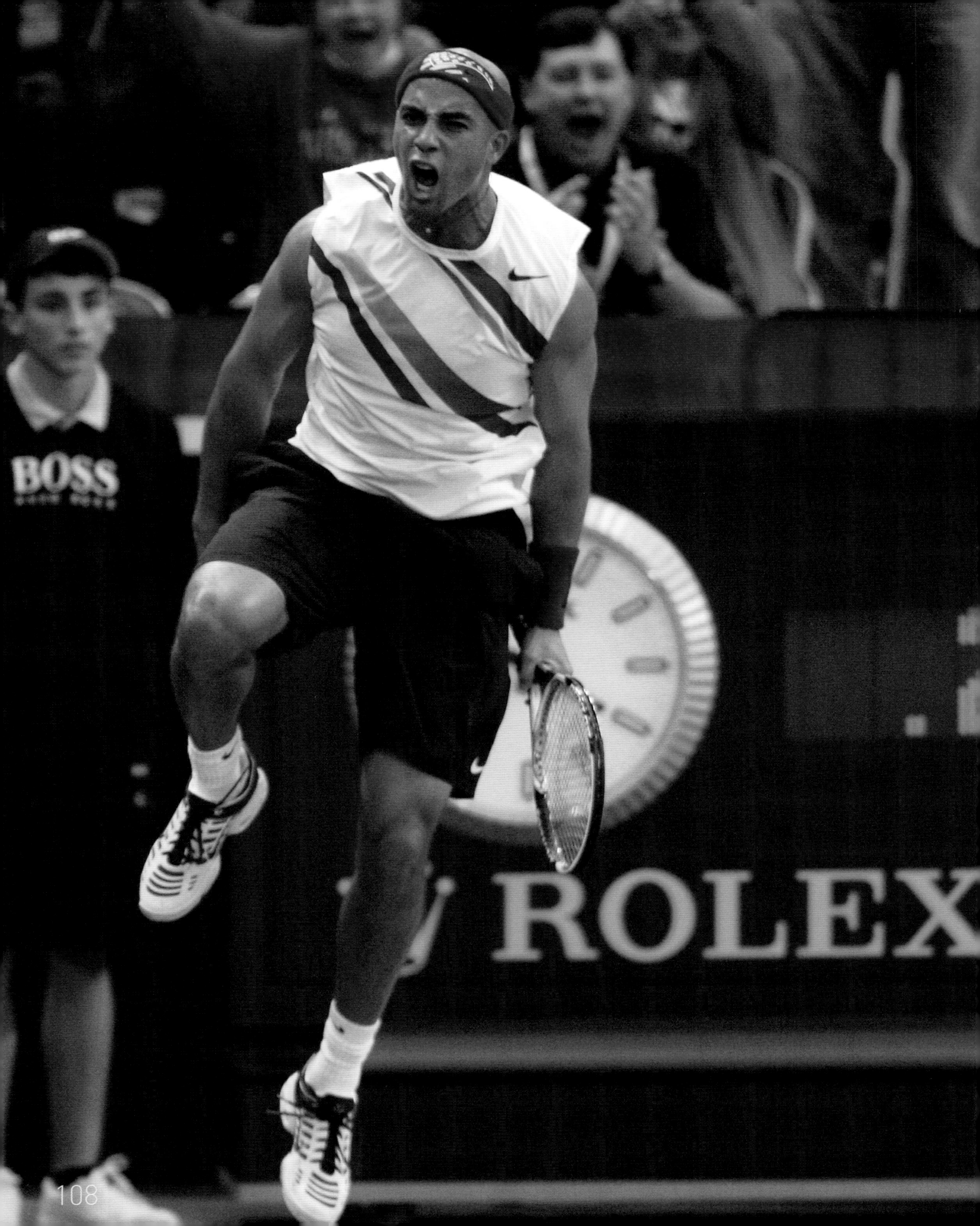
BOSS
ROLEX

USA v RUSSIA CONTINUED

guys cheering for each other. It made me fall in love with Davis Cup, and just made me want to be a part of it." Three years earlier he had led the American team into the final on the red clay of Seville, where his best efforts weren't quite good enough against the burgeoning Rafael Nadal and the Davis Cup's player of 2004, Carlos Moya. This time he was coming full circle after his baptism in 1992, and he was not going to be knocked off track.

Only once in his 6–4, 6–4, 6–2 win did Roddick wobble. After missing a set point at 5–3 on the Tursunov serve, he held six on his own in the tenth game of the match. He had eaten into Tursunov's confidence with a patient backcourt game that involved a number of heavily sliced backhands, but on the point of taking the set, Tursunov threw the tactic back at Roddick with some gently lofted forehands and paceless flat backhands. The rallies got longer and more cat-and-mouse. Tursunov saved Roddick's fourth set point with the help of a successful appeal to the electronic official review. It looked all set to become a contest.

But when Roddick thundered down an unreturnable serve to convert his eighth set point, he extinguished Tursunov's resistance. Tursunov later said he was "afraid to play," meaning too scared to make mistakes to play his natural aggressive game. He was a shade harsh on himself. He should take credit for at least trying different things, but Roddick handled the situation so much better. He too was nervous, his movement hampered in the opening set. But this was his destiny. He played a smarter match than his opponent and he notched up the USA's first point before two hours had been played.

If Russia was to make any headway in the final, Youzhny had to beat James Blake in the second singles. Given the Davis Cup prowess of Roddick and the Bryans' status as the runaway world No. 1 pair, Blake had been targeted all year as the Americans' weak link, despite starting the year ranked No. 4 and ending it at 13. Tomas Berdych had beaten him on the opening day of the first-round tie in Ostrava; Thomas Johansson had beaten him on the first day of the semifinal in Gothenburg. And after a disappointing last two months of the year following a morale-sapping five-set defeat to Tommy Haas at the US Open, Blake came to Portland as the player with most doubt surrounding him.

He claimed not to be worried by the pressure, and there was no question about the legitimacy of his place in the U.S. team. But the doubters were circling the Blake–Youzhny match, just waiting for the moment when Blake would falter. He did—but recovered to see off the doubters, keeping his cool at the point where Youzhny was making his move toward another memorable Davis Cup victory.

Riding the wave of Roddick's win, Blake raced out of the block, breaking Youzhny in the second game and again early in the second set. Only then did the Russian banish the nerves that had hampered him for the first forty-five minutes and, had he broken for a second successive time at 3–2, he might have run away with the second set. But Blake hung in, took it in the tiebreak and seemed on course to deprive the Russians of a single first-day set.

Youzhny, however, is one of those players who grows stronger the longer a match wears on, especially in Davis Cup. He refused to get downcast by the size of the task now facing him and won the third set in the tiebreak, finding Blake's backhand with increasing

Pictured opposite:

James Blake (USA)

Pictured from top:

Mikhail Youzhny (RUS)

Russian fans in Portland

Patrick McEnroe (USA)

regularity. Blake's forehand was still his lethal weapon, firing winners from all parts of the court, but the weaker wing was becoming more exposed. And Youzhny was getting into Blake's head.

But then the Russian played a poor game at 4–4, and suddenly Blake was serving for the match. This was his moment, but he handed it to the doubters. Youzhny played one of his best returning games of the match, Blake threw in a couple of unforced errors, and the Russian broke to 15 to level the fourth set at 5–5. The match had the hallmarks of a Youzhny classic, and the specter of Blake's five-set defeat to Fernando Gonzalez in the 2006 quarterfinals, when he served for the match in the third set only to lose in five, looked like it might come back to haunt him.

When Youzhny took an early minibreak in the fourth-set tiebreak, a fifth set seemed likely. But Blake regrouped and seized on Youzhny's rush of blood at 3–4 when the Russian played an ill-advised drop shot with such poor execution that the ball barely reached the net. Blake was suddenly in control and, with no return of nerves, banished his demons with a 6–3, 7–6(4), 6–7(3), 7–6(3) victory.

When asked in an on-court interview how it felt to have won, Blake said: "Euphoria: my vocabulary isn't big enough to describe how great this feels. To have my family here, to have my brother and mother in the front row, to have all my friends flying out here to see me, and to have twelve thousand screaming fans here. Questions about whether or not I'd be able to get through this and tough situations, how many live matches I've won this year, it means nothing at this point."

He may have been targeted as the weak link, but Blake is one of the strongest characters in tennis. His annus horribilis of 2004—when he broke his neck colliding with a net post, contracted a form of shingles, and saw his father die rapidly of cancer—had added fortitude to his already eloquent personality. His description of this difficult period of his life came out in the form of a book, Breaking Back, published in July 2007, which earned the likeable former Harvard student a place in the realms of best-selling authors.

In his moment of triumph, he exchanged high fives and hugs with his teammates, and before embarking on a round of on-court postmatch interviews, beckoned his mother, Betty, to come over for a warm embrace by the side of the court. "We've been through a lot," he explained, "She's been through a lot more than me, and it's so fun to see her happy. She's been through so many of these, I've given her a million gray hairs from all my tennis matches, and to see her smiling means so much to me. I wanted to tell her that I love her and how much she meant to me and how she got me here."

Though history will record that a high forehand volley from the racket of Bob Bryan sealed the Davis Cup for the Americans, it was Blake's win that effectively ended Russian hopes. There was simply no viable way back after that. In the run-up to the final, the doubles seemed the one banker for the Americans, such was the dominance of Bob and Mike Bryan in the world of men's doubles. Their lead in the year-end rankings over the year's second-best pair, Mark Knowles and Daniel Nestor, was much greater than Roger Federer's singles lead over the second-ranked Rafael Nadal. And with Russia parading four singles players without an obvious doubles combination, the visitors' only hope seemed to lie in some freak injury afflicting one of the twins.

Pictured from top:

Bob and Mike Bryan (USA)

Nikolay Davydenko and Igor Andreev (RUS)

Pictured opposite:

Andy Roddick leaps the net to congratulate

Bob and Mike Bryan (USA)

Pictured from top:
Captain Patrick McEnroe and Billie Jean King (USA)
American fans in Portland (USA)
Pictured opposite from top:
Portland's Memorial Coliseum
American team celebrates victory

USA v RUSSIA CONTINUED

Indeed there was no hope but it would be wrong to gloss over the display posted by Andreev and Davydenko in the Bryans' 7–6(4), 6–4, 6–2 win. The Russians again showed why they had won a tour doubles title three years earlier with a measured display of backcourt tennis that, for a set at least, matched what the Bryans could offer. The Russians even had the temerity to take a 3–1 lead in the first-set tiebreak, at which point the twins were facing the prospect of what would have been only their second dropped set of the year. But the whiff of danger brought out the best in them, and five straight points turned the tiebreak around, and with it the match.

After the set had gone, the Russians lost a little heart. Davydenko, who claimed to have overcome an elbow injury that had affected his serve so badly that two umpires in tour matches had suggested he wasn't trying hard enough, was clearly serving well below full pace, and it was he who dropped his serve three times as the Bryans took a stranglehold. The third of them took the USA to within a game of the title. At 40–30, they executed a move they have done several thousand times, but never to such valuable effect: Mike served into the body of Davydenko, Davydenko couldn't get enough angle on his return, and Bob pounced with a high forehand volley to secure the Davis Cup for America.

Cue wild celebrations among the American team. Cue passionate rejoicing among most of the crowd of twelve thousand in the Memorial Coliseum. Cue the release of red, white, and blue streamers from the dark void of the Coliseum's roof. Cue the rehabilitation of American team tennis following the end of the golden era of Courier, Agassi, Sampras, Chang, and Martin.

Irrespective of one's nationality, there were many reasons to be happy for the Americans that afternoon. Four twenty-something players, for whom a downside of tennis was that it was primarily an individual sport, had bonded into a unit that had become a second family to all of them and had won the biggest prize in international team competition. And the man who had shaped that team ethic sat quietly at the side of the court watching the celebrations. It was an emotional moment for Patrick McEnroe—his wife, Melissa Errico, had sung the U.S. national anthem at the start of play, his daughter, Victoria, whose birth had forced him to miss the 2006 quarterfinal, was courtside, and he had finally achieved something his illustrious elder brother John had never done—captain a winning Davis Cup team.

Typical for the man, he had to be coaxed into accepting any credit. When asked about having achieved something John hadn't, he would only highlight the sterling contribution John made in the Davis Cup. He talked about his seven years as Davis Cup captain as a "labor of love." And when, at a postmatch news conference oozing the aroma of newly sprayed champagne, McEnroe was asked whether this was his best feeling in tennis, he again had to be helped out of his second-line role by the ecstatic Andy Roddick. "You know it's not about me; it's about this whole group of guys," McEnroe said, only to be interrupted by Roddick screaming "Say yes!"

"Yes it is!" responded McEnroe in his only ebullient gesture of the weekend.

If Roddick had enjoyed a little alcohol in his moment of triumph, he wasn't in the mood to limit his intake when his obligations were over. He got to bed around five

Pictured from top:

The American team with the Davis Cup trophy

The Russian team at the trophy presentation ceremony

Pictured opposite:

The American team celebrates victory

USA v RUSSIA CONTINUED

o'clock in the small hours of Sunday, and when the Bryan twins saw him later that morning, they knew instantly that one of them would have to step in for the dead rubber. In the on-court team presentation on the final day, Roddick walked in his slippers through the drums and fireworks that greeted him, looking for all the world as if he was inside the drums, and the fireworks were going off inside his head.

In his place, Bob put up a creditable showing in his 6–3, 7–6(4) defeat to Andreev, and the record books will show a 4–1 victory for the Americans after James Blake beat Dmitry Tursunov 1–6, 6–3, 7–5. Blake began the match with his mouth full of popcorn he had swiped from a bucket on the lap of his non-playing teammate, Robby Ginepri. But the real winner on the final day was the crowd. While the television sports presenters had sounded somewhat incredulous in reporting that the dead rubbers would actually be played, the knowledgeable American fans turned out in full numbers for the presentation day and were rewarded with some entertaining tennis.

The crowd took its share of the credit in the final speeches, both sides crediting the way the spectators had been scrupulously fair in their partisanship. And alluding to the wider statesmanlike role of top sports stars, McEnroe told the crowd: "Over my seven years as captain, it hasn't always been easy to represent the USA in certain parts of the world, but these guys have done so with great class and it's been a privilege for me to have been with them."

McEnroe also had a playful dig at the somewhat class-less attire in which the Russian team attended the official dinner. While the American team turned up dressed slickly in dark suits and gray ties, the Russians turned up in more casual wear, a point clearly of some embarrassment to the besuited Shamil Tarpischev. "We mean no disrespect by the way we are dressed," he said. "We do have suits, but like in the days of the old Soviet Union, they sent them all in the same size." The assembled Davis Cup community roared its approval and, after that, any sartorial indiscretions were happily forgiven.

Through an alcoholic haze, several players took to the microphone. Igor Andreev said the spirit and harmony fostered by the Davis Cup was "just great"; Dmitry Tursunov asked to be considered an international citizen rather than an Americanized Russian or a Russian American; Patrick McEnroe admitted that his brother was in attendance (Mark, not John, who was preparing for a seniors tour event in London); and the patriarch and matriarch of the McEnroe dynasty, Kay and John Sr., enjoyed the moment five days before their fiftieth wedding anniversary. Slickly organized it was not, but international friendship doesn't always follow the dictates of stage-managed social occasions.

Outside, the rain came cascading down from the Cascades. The drought in American team tennis fortunes was over, and Dwight Davis's competition, while not pushing football and basketball off the sports pages, was a bigger part of the American sporting psyche than it had been a few days earlier. ●

PLASYER OF THE YEAR

Name Andy Roddick
Born 30 August 1982 in Omaha, Nebraska, USA
Turned professional 2000

HISTORY MAY YET BE VERY UNKIND TO ANDY RODDICK. His US Open title and thirteen weeks at the top of the rankings caught the period just before Roger Federer's dominance, and there are those who harbor the opinion that, but for Federer's tardiness in reaching his full potential, Roddick would never have scaled the heights he reached in 2003.

Whether or not that is fair, in the Davis Cup—a competition that does strange things to rankings—Roddick has grown into a colossus. His enthusiasm for the competition is unquestioned, but he has turned a mediocre start into a formidable record, to the point where, by the end of 2007, he had played nine matches for the USA to win a tie, and won them all.

His love affair with the Davis Cup began as a ten-year-old at the 1992 final, when his mother got tickets through their tennis club. Andy was smitten with the team variant of tennis, a love affair that was enhanced when he was called up as practice partner for the 2000 quarterfinal in Los Angeles, when John McEnroe was the captain and had coaxed back Pete Sampras and Andre Agassi. "I didn't really fit in," Roddick recalls of that breakthrough experience. "We had Pete and Andre, John McEnroe as captain, two top-10 doubles players, and the other practice partner was Todd Martin, who was about seven in the world. It was a pretty humbling experience, but huge for me. I went back to my tournaments feeling so much more confident."

Less than a year later, Roddick made his Davis Cup debut. History records that it was in a dead rubber in Basel, after Roger Federer had won three points to see Switzerland to a 3–1 victory in Patrick McEnroe's first tie as captain. But McEnroe has since admitted that he would have given Roddick his debut even if the fifth rubber had been live, such was his confidence in the enthusiasm of the Nebraskan-born Texan.

Although Roddick beat George Bastl in Basel, his early Davis Cup performances were mixed. "I've had to learn to become more comfortable in Davis Cup," he says. "A lot of the credit goes to my teammates who have given me support. It means I'm so much more relaxed out there now than I was at the beginning."

Roddick is a complex character. The youngest of three brothers—with considerable age gaps between the three—he has always been a mixture of the sassy teenager and the class act waiting to break out. This writer first spoke with Roddick at the ITF World Champions Dinner that honored him for being the best junior of 2000. Surrounded by older men in dinner suits and bow ties, he was both dignified and uncomfortable. He knew how to behave and could be charming, but seemed more comfortable in the too-cool-to-be-kind youth scene.

Over the years, many in the tennis world—especially in the media—have found Roddick's transition out of that youth culture to be taking longer than expected. For a man of such natural charm, he can be bitingly monosyllabic at times and can assume an inherent aggressiveness and stupidity in questions put to him that are seldom intended.

Yet there were signs that his team triumph of 2007 was bringing more of his class act out. His dignity and warmth in the way he approached the Davis Cup final were marked, both at the Tennis Masters Cup in Shanghai two weeks earlier and in the days leading up to the final. If dignity establishes a powerful root, Andy Roddick will become a delightful man to be around—and a shoo-in as U.S. Davis Cup captain sometime in the future. ●

Pictured opposite:

Andy Roddick with Bob Bryan

BACKSTAGE AT THE FINAL

Busy times behind the scenes at the Davis Cup by BNP Paribas Final

WORLD GROUP

First Round 9-11 February

Russia defeated Chile 3-2, La Serena, CHI, Clay (O): Marat Safin (RUS) d. Nicolas Massu (CHI) 63 62 62; Igor Andreev (RUS) d. Fernando Gonzalez (CHI) 46 64 63 62; Fernando Gonzalez/ Nicolas Massu (CHI) d. Igor Andreev/Marat Safin (RUS) 76(3) 63 64; Fernando Gonzalez (CHI) d. Marat Safin (RUS) 63 75 64; Igor Andreev (RUS) d. Nicolas Massu (CHI) 62 61 67(1) 64.

France defeated Romania 4-1, Clermont-Ferrand, FRA, Carpet (I): Richard Gasquet (FRA) d. Victor Hanescu (ROU) 75 62 62; Sebastien Grosjean (FRA) d. Andrei Pavel (ROU) 46 57 63 61 62; Florin Mergea/Horia Tecau (ROU) d. Arnaud Clement/Michael Llodra (FRA) 36 75 75 67(3) 119; Richard Gasquet (FRA) d. Andrei Pavel (ROU) 63 62 75; Arnaud Clement (FRA) d. Florin Mergea (ROU) 75 76(3).

Germany defeated Croatia 3-2, Krefeld, GER, Hard (I): Tommy Haas (GER) d. Mario Ancic (CRO) 26 64 64 64; Ivan Ljubicic (CRO) d. Benjamin Becker (GER) 67(4) 64 62 63; Michael Kohlmann/Alexander Waske (GER) d. Mario Ancic/Ivan Ljubicic (CRO) 64 62 76(5); Tommy Haas (GER) d. Ivan Ljubicic (CRO) 62 76(7) 64; Marin Cilic (CRO) d. Benjamin Becker (GER) 64 16 61.

Belgium defeated Australia 3-2, Liege, BEL, Clay (I): Kristof Vliegen (BEL) d. Lleyton Hewitt (AUS) 46 64 36 63 64; Olivier Rochus (BEL) d. Chris Guccione (AUS) 36 75 62 63; Paul Hanley/ Lleyton Hewitt (AUS) d. Olivier Rochus/Kristof Vliegen (BEL) 62 64 62; Lleyton Hewitt (AUS) d. Olivier Rochus (BEL) 62 63 67(4) 36 61; Kristof Vliegen (BEL) d. Chris Guccione (AUS) 64 64 64.

USA defeated Czech Republic 4-1, Ostrava, CZE, Clay (I): Andy Roddick (USA) d. Ivo Minar (CZE) 64 46 62 63; Tomas Berdych (CZE) d. James Blake (USA) 61 26 75 75; Bob Bryan/Mike Bryan (USA) d. Lukas Dlouhy/Pavel Vizner (CZE) 64 46 64 64; Andy Roddick (USA) d. Tomas Berdych (CZE) 46 63 62 76(4); Bob Bryan (USA) d. Lukas Dlouhy (CZE) 75 64.

Spain defeated Switzerland 3-2, Geneva, SUI, Carpet (I): Marco Chiudinelli (SUI) d. Fernando Verdasco (ESP) 63 64 36 76(2); David Ferrer (ESP) d. Stephane Bohli (SUI) 63 62 62; Feliciano Lopez/Fernando Verdasco (ESP) d. Yves Allegro/Marco Chiudinelli (SUI) 76(5) 67(3) 67(2) 61 1210; Fernando Verdasco (ESP) d. Stephane Bohli (SUI) 63 63 62; Marco Chiudinelli (SUI) d. David Ferrer (ESP) 36 63 63.

Sweden defeated Belarus 3-2, Minsk, BLR, Carpet (I): Robin Soderling (SWE) d. Vladimir Voltchkov (BLR) 63 76(3) 61; Thomas Johansson (SWE) d. Max Mirnyi (BLR) 64 64 64; Max Mirnyi/ Vladimir Voltchkov (BLR) d. Simon Aspelin/Jonas Bjorkman (SWE) 75 46 75 63; Robin Soderling (SWE) d. Max Mirnyi (BLR) 67(8) 75 67(8) 76(3) 63; Vladimir Voltchkov (BLR) d. Thomas Johansson (SWE) 64 75.

Argentina defeated Austria 4-1, Linz, AUT, Carpet (I): Jose Acasuso (ARG) d. Stefan Koubek (AUT) 76(6) 61 64; Guillermo Canas (ARG) d. Jurgen Melzer (AUT) 76(6) 62 64; Julian Knowle/ Jurgen Melzer (AUT) d. Jose Acasuso/Sebastian Prieto (ARG) 63 67(2) 61 75; Juan-Martin Del Potro (ARG) d. Jurgen Melzer (AUT) 76(4) 36 64 46 62; Guillermo Canas (ARG) d. Alexander Peya (AUT) 46 61 64.

Quarterfinals 6-8 April

Russia defeated France 3-2, Moscow, RUS, Clay (I): Paul-Henri Mathieu (FRA) d. Nikolay Davydenko (RUS) 26 62 61 75; Mikhail Youzhny (RUS) d. Richard Gasquet (FRA) 62 63 67(8) 57 86; Igor Andreev/Nikolay Davydenko (RUS) d. Sebastien Grosjean/Michael Llodra (FRA) 36 75 63 63 63; Sebastien Grosjean (FRA) d. Igor Andreev (RUS) 75 46 26 63 64; Marat Safin (RUS) d. Paul-Henri Mathieu (FRA) 76(3) 63 62.

Germany defeated Belgium 3-2, Ostend, BEL, Clay (I): Tommy Haas (GER) d. Kristof Vliegen (BEL) 67(4) 75 64 62; Philipp Kohlschreiber (GER) d. Olivier Rochus (BEL) 63 75 76(4); Michael Kohlmann/Alexander Waske (GER) d. Christophe Rochus/Olivier Rochus (BEL) 46 62 63 61; Christophe Rochus (BEL) d. Michael Kohlmann (GER) 36 64 64; Dick Norman (BEL) d. Philipp Kohlschreiber (GER) 62 63.

USA defeated Spain 4-1, Winston-Salem, NC, USA, Hard (I): James Blake (USA) d. Tommy Robredo (ESP) 64 63 64; Andy Roddick (USA) d. Fernando Verdasco (ESP) 76(5) 61 64; Bob Bryan/Mike Bryan (USA) d. Feliciano Lopez/Fernando Verdasco (ESP) 75 63 36 76(5); Tommy Robredo (ESP) d. Bob Bryan (USA) 64 64; James Blake (USA) d. Feliciano Lopez (ESP) 63 76(3).

Sweden defeated Argentina 4-1, Gothenburg, SWE, Carpet (I): Thomas Johansson (SWE) d. David Nalbandian (ARG) 67(3) 76(2) 62 76(0); Robin Soderling (SWE) d. Juan-Martin Del Potro (ARG) 76(4) 76(4) 64; Jonas Bjorkman/Thomas Johansson (SWE) d. Guillermo Canas/David Nalbandian (ARG) 46 76(4) 62 63; Jonas Bjorkman (SWE) d. Sebastian Prieto (ARG) 61 62; Juan-Martin Del Potro (ARG) d. Robert Lindstedt (SWE) 76(7) 64.

Semifinals 21-23 September

Russia defeated Germany 3-2, Moscow, RUS, Clay (I): Igor Andreev (RUS) d. Tommy Haas (GER) 62 62 62; Philipp Kohlschreiber (GER) d. Nikolay Davydenko (RUS) 67(5) 62 46 75; Philipp Petzschner/Alexander Waske (GER) d. Dmitry Tursunov/Mikhail Youzhny (RUS) 63 36 76(4) 76(5); Mikhail Youzhny (RUS) d. Philipp Petzschner (GER) 64 64 36 63; Igor Andreev (RUS) d. Philipp Kohlschreiber (GER) 63 36 60 63.

USA defeated Sweden 4-1, Gothenburg, SWE, Carpet (I): Andy Roddick (USA) d. Joachim Johansson (SWE) 76(4) 76(3) 62; Thomas Johansson (SWE) d. James Blake (USA) 64 62 36 63; Bob Bryan/Mike Bryan (USA) d. Simon Aspelin/Jonas Bjorkman (SWE) 76(11) 62 63; Andy Roddick (USA) d. Jonas Bjorkman (SWE) 62 76(3) 64; James Blake (USA) d. Simon Aspelin (SWE) 61 63.

Final 31 November-2 December

USA defeated Russia 4-1; Portland, OR, USA, Hard (I): Andy Roddick (USA) d. Dmitry Tursunov (RUS) 64 64 62; James Blake (USA) d. Mikhail Youzhny (RUS) 63 76(4) 67(3) 76(3); Bob Bryan/Mike Bryan (USA) d. Igor Andreev/Nikolay Davydenko (RUS) 76(4) 64 62; Igor Andreev (RUS) d. Bob Bryan (USA) 63 76(4); James Blake (USA) d. Dmitry Tursunov (RUS) 16 63 75.

World Group Play-offs 21-23 September

Israel defeated Chile 3-2, Ramat Hasharon, ISR, Hard (O): Dudi Sela (ISR) d. Nicolas Massu (CHI) 63 64 67(3) 64; Fernando Gonzalez (CHI) d. Noam Okun (ISR) 46 63 75 64; Jonathan Erlich/Andy Ram (ISR) d. Fernando Gonzalez/Nicolas Massu (CHI) 26 76(1) 62 36 108; Dudi Sela (ISR) d. Fernando Gonzalez (CHI) 46 76(5) 57 76(7) 63; Paul Capdeville (CHI) d. Noam Okun (ISR) 21 ret.

Serbia defeated Australia 4-1, Belgrade, SRB, Clay (I): Novak Djokovic (SRB) d. Peter Luczak (AUS) 61 64 62; Lleyton Hewitt (AUS) d. Janko Tipsarevic (SRB) 62 36 46 61 61; Novak Djokovic/ Nenad Zimonjic (SRB) d. Paul Hanley/Lleyton Hewitt (AUS) 36 64 63 62; Novak Djokovic (SRB) d. Chris Guccione (AUS) 63 76(3) 76(5); Boris Pashanski (SRB) d. Peter Luczak (AUS) 46 63 61.

Austria defeated Brazil 4-1: Innsbruck, AUT, Hard (I): Jurgen Melzer (AUT) d. Thomaz Bellucci (BRA) 64 64 64; Stefan Koubek (AUT) d. Ricardo Mello (BRA) 62 63 63; Julian Knowle/ Jurgen Melzer (AUT) d. Gustavo Kuerten/Andre Sa (BRA) 61 61 64; Jurgen Melzer (AUT) d. Ricardo Mello (BRA) 36 64 75; Andre Sa (BRA) d. Werner Eschauer (AUT) 64 63.

Peru defeated Belarus 4-1, Lima, PER, Clay (O): Ivan Miranda (PER) d. Max Mirnyi (BLR) 64 36 76(6) 64; Luis Horna (PER) d. Vladimir Voltchkov (BLR) 36 67(4) 64 64 62; Max Mirnyi/ Vladimir Voltchkov (BLR) d. Ivan Miranda/Matias Silva (PER) 63 75 62; Luis Horna (PER) d. Max Mirnyi (BLR) 64 75 46 76(4); Matias Silva (PER) d. Andrei Karatchenia (BLR) 64 64.

Great Britain defeated Croatia 4-1, London, GBR, Grass (O): Andy Murray (GBR) d. Marin Cilic (CRO) 36 64 62 46 63; Tim Henman (GBR) d. Roko Karanusic (CRO) 64 63 63; Tim Henman/ Jamie Murray (GBR) d. Marin Cilic/Lovro Zovko (CRO) 46 64 76(3) 75; Andy Murray (GBR) d. Roko Karanusic (CRO) 64 76(4); Marin Cilic (CRO) d. Jamie Baker (GBR) 64 64.

Czech Republic defeated Switzerland 3-2, Prague, CZE, Carpet (I): Roger Federer (SUI) d. Radek Stepanek (CZE) 63 62 67(4) 76(5); Tomas Berdych (CZE) d. Stanislas Wawrinka (SUI) 76(2) 64 75; Tomas Berdych/Radek Stepanek (CZE) d. Yves Allegro/Roger Federer (SUI) 36 57 76(7) 64 64; Roger Federer (SUI) d. Tomas Berdych (CZE) 76(5) 76(10) 63; Radek Stepanek (CZE) d. Stanislas Wawrinka (SUI) 76(3) 63 76(4).

Romania defeated Japan 3-2, Osaka, JPN, Carpet (I): Takao Suzuki (JPN) d. Victor Hanescu (ROU) 76(4) 61 76(4); Andrei Pavel (ROU) d. Go Soeda (JPN) 63 67(7) 75 63; Satoshi Iwabuchi/ Takao Suzuki (JPN) d. Florin Mergea/Horia Tecau (ROU) 64 64 64; Andrei Pavel (ROU) d. Takao Suzuki (JPN) 67(6) 67(1) 61 64 64; Victor Hanescu (ROU) d. Go Soeda (JPN) 63 57 76(6) 76(3).

Korea, Rep. defeated Slovak Republic 3-2, Bratislava, SVK, Clay (I): Hyung-Taik Lee (KOR) d. Martin Klizan (SVK) 63 60 61; Lukas Lacko (SVK) d. Woong-Sun Jun (KOR) 63 62 76(2); Kyu-Tae Im/Hyung-Taik Lee (KOR) d. Lukas Lacko/Michal Mertinak (SVK) 60 63 62; Hyung-Taik Lee (KOR) d. Lukas Lacko (SVK) 63 63 46 61; Michal Mertinak (SVK) d. Jae-Sung An (KOR) 63 62.

GROUP I

Americas Zone
First Round 9-11 February

Peru defeated Venezuela 3-2, Asia, PER, Clay (O): Luis Horna (PER) d. Jhonnatan Medina-Alvarez (VEN) 63 64 26 64; Ivan Miranda (PER) d. Yohny Romero (VEN) 61 62 61; Ivan Miranda/Matias Silva (PER) d. David Navarrete/Yohny Romero (VEN) 63 63 16 67(1) 64; Roman Recarte (VEN) d. Mauricio Echazu (PER) 46 75 62; Jhonnatan Medina-Alvarez (VEN) d. Matias Silva (PER) 63 63.

Canada defeated Colombia 5-0, Calgary, CAN, Carpet (I): Frank Dancevic (CAN) d. Santiago Giraldo (COL) 62 64 63; Frederic Niemeyer (CAN) d. Alejandro Falla (COL) 60 76(5) 63; Daniel Nestor/Frederic Niemeyer (CAN) d. Alejandro Falla/Carlos Salamanca (COL) 76(2) 62 63; Frank Dancevic (CAN) d. Pablo Gonzalez (COL) 61 75; Peter Polansky (CAN) d. Carlos Salamanca (COL) 76(4) 64.

Second Round 6-8 April

Peru defeated Mexico 3-2, Asia, PER, Clay (O): Luis Horna (PER) d. Daniel Garza (MEX) 64 76(8) 26 63; Ivan Miranda (PER) d. Santiago Gonzalez (MEX) 64 36 61 57 86; Luis Horna/Ivan Miranda (PER) d. Santiago Gonzalez/Antonio Ruiz-Rosales (MEX) 61 63 61; Juan-Manuel Elizondo (MEX) d. Matias Silva (PER) 64 63; Daniel Garza (MEX) d. Mauricio Echazu (PER) 46 61 64.

Brazil defeated Canada 3-1, Florianopolis, BRA, Clay (O): Ricardo Mello (BRA) d. Frank Dancevic (CAN) 36 67(7) 63 63 119; Flavio Saretta (BRA) d. Frederic Niemeyer (CAN) 64 67(6) 62 61; Daniel Nestor/Frederic Niemeyer (CAN) d. Gustavo Kuerten/Andre Sa (BRA) 46 63 64 76(4); Flavio Saretta (BRA) d. Peter Polansky (CAN) 16 62 75 61.

Brazil and Peru advanced to World Group Play-offs on 21-23 September 2007.

First Round Relegation Play-off 20-22 July

Mexico defeated Venezuela 5-0, Edo de Mexico, MEX, Hard (O): Daniel Garza (MEX) d. Yohny Romero (VEN) 64 46 62 46 63; Santiago Gonzalez (MEX) d. Jhonnatan Medina-Alvarez (VEN) 63 62 62; Daniel Garza/Santiago Gonzalez (MEX) d. Roberto Maytin/Daniel Vallverdu (VEN) 64 75 36 46 62; Daniel Garza (MEX) d. Daniel Vallverdu (VEN) 76(5) 61; Juan-Manuel Elizondo (MEX) d. Roberto Maytin (VEN) 60 61.

Second Round Relegation Play-off 21-23 September

Colombia defeated Venezuela 4-1, Valencia, VEN, Hard (O): Santiago Giraldo (COL) d. Yohny Romero (VEN) 63 63 64; Alejandro Falla (COL) d. Jhonnatan Medina-Alvarez (VEN) 62 64 76(4); Yohny Romero/Daniel Vallverdu (VEN) d. Alejandro Falla/Carlos Salamanca (COL) 76(5) 16 63 76(7); Alejandro Falla (COL) d. Yohny Romero (VEN) 60 62 62; Michael Quintero (COL) d. Jhonnatan Medina-Alvarez (VEN) 63 63.

Venezuela relegated to Americas Zone Group II in 2008.

Asia/Oceania Zone
First Round 9-11 February

Thailand defeated Chinese Taipei 3-2, Taipei County, TPE, Carpet (I): Danai Udomchoke (THA) d. Hsin-Han Lee (TPE) 61 61 62; Ti Chen (TPE) d. Weerapat Doakmaiklee (THA) 76(1) 67(10) 61 63; Ti Chen/Chu-Huan Yi (TPE) d. Sanchai Ratiwatana/Sonchat Ratiwatana (THA) 63 63 63; Danai Udomchoke (THA) d. Tai-Wei Liu (TPE) 60 61 63; Sonchat Ratiwatana (THA) d. Hsin-Han Lee (TPE) 76(7) 64 63.

Japan defeated China, P.R. 4-1, Beijing, CHN, Hard (I): Yuichi Sugita (JPN) d. Xin-Yuan Yu (CHN) 76(5) 06 67(2) 63 64; Go Soeda (JPN) d. Peng Sun (CHN) 64 64 76(7); Satoshi Iwabuchi/Takao Suzuki (JPN) d. Xin-Yuan Yu/Shao-Xuan Zeng (CHN) 63 67(6) 63 61; Go Soeda (JPN) d. Xin-Yuan Yu (CHN) 63 64; Peng Sun (CHN) d. Yuichi Sugita (JPN) 63 76(1).

Uzbekistan defeated India 4-1, Namangan, UZB, Clay (I): Denis Istomin (UZB) d. Vivek Shokeen (IND) 61 63 63; Farrukh Dustov (UZB) d. Karan Rastogi (IND) 63 63 64; Leander Paes/Sunil-Kumar Sipaeya (IND) d. Farrukh Dustov/Denis Istomin (UZB) 64 64 36 46 63; Denis Istomin (UZB) d. Karan Rastogi (IND) 76(2) 75 61; Murad Inoyatov (UZB) d. Vivek Shokeen (IND) 63 46 76(3).

Korea, Rep. defeated Kazakhstan 5-0, Chuncheon-si, KOR, Carpet (I): Woong-Sun Jun (KOR) d. Alexei Kedryuk (KAZ) 64 61 64; Hyung-Taik Lee (KOR) d. Syrym Abdukhalikov (KAZ) 62 62 62; Woong-Sun Jun/Hyung-Taik Lee (KOR) d. Alexei Kedryuk/Dmitriy Makeyev (KAZ) 61 75 62; Sun-Yong Kim (KOR) d. Dmitriy Makeyev (KAZ) 63 61; Jae-Sung An (KOR) d. Syrym Abdukhalikov (KAZ) 64 61.

Second Round 6-8 April

Japan defeated Thailand 5-0, Osaka, JPN, Carpet (I): Go Soeda (JPN) d. Kittiphong Wachiramanowong (THA) 61 62 62; Takao Suzuki (JPN) d. Weerapat Doakmaiklee (THA) 64 62 63; Satoshi Iwabuchi/Takao Suzuki (JPN) d. Sanchai Ratiwatana/Sonchat Ratiwatana (THA) 63 64 26 64; Go Soeda (JPN) d. Weerapat Doakmaiklee (THA) 61 62; Yuichi Sugita (JPN) d. Kittiphong Wachiramanowong (THA) 62 64.

Korea, Rep. defeated Uzbekistan 5-0, Seoul, KOR, Hard (O): Kyu-Tae Im (KOR) d. Farrukh Dustov (UZB) 60 62 46 75; Hyung-Taik Lee (KOR) d. Denis Istomin (UZB) 63 62 62; Jae-Sung An/Woong-Sun Jun (KOR) d. Farrukh Dustov/Denis Istomin (UZB) 61 63 61; Woong-Sun Jun (KOR) d. Sarvar Ikramov (UZB) 75 64; Jae-Sung An (KOR) d. Vaja Uzakov (UZB) 61 62.

Japan and Korea, Rep. advanced to World Group Play-offs on 21-23 September 2007.

First Round Relegation Play-offs 6-8 April

Chinese Taipei defeated China, P.R. 3-2, Taipei, TPE, Carpet (I): Yen-Hsun Lu (TPE) d. Peng Sun (CHN) 36 62 36 64 62; Yeu-Tzuoo Wang (TPE) d. Xin-Yuan Yu (CHN) 63 62 64; Xin-Yuan Yu/Shao-Xuan Zeng (CHN) d. Ti Chen/Chu-Huan Yi (TPE) 76(7) 46 75 63; Xin-Yuan Yu (CHN) d. Yen-Hsun Lu (TPE) 64 75 26 76(4); Yeu-Tzuoo Wang (TPE) d. Peng Sun (CHN) 64 75 63.

India defeated Kazakhstan 3-2, Almaty, KAZ, Hard (I): Rohan Bopanna (IND) d. Dmitriy Makeyev (KAZ) 62 61 62; Alexei Kedryuk (KAZ) d. Karan Rastogi (IND) 64 64 36 76(2); Rohan Bopanna/Leander Paes (IND) d. Alexei Kedryuk/Dmitriy Makeyev (KAZ) 62 62 62; Alexei Kedryuk (KAZ) d. Rohan Bopanna (IND) 64 64 36 46 64; Leander Paes (IND) d. Dmitriy Makeyev (KAZ) 67(4) 64 64 64.

Second Round Relegation Play-off 21-23 September

Kazakhstan defeated China, P.R. 3-2, Almaty, KAZ, Hard (I): Alexei Kedryuk (KAZ) d. Peng Sun (CHN) 76(3) 76(4) 63; Syrym Abdukhalikov (KAZ) d. Xin-Yuan Yu (CHN) 76(5) 63 26 75; Xin-Yuan Yu/Shao-Xuan Zeng (CHN) d. Syrym Abdukhalikov/Alexey Kedryuk (KAZ) 63 62 67(6) 75; Alexey Kedryuk (KAZ) d. Xin-Yuan Yu (CHN) 62 63 76(2); Peng Sun (CHN) d. Stanislav Bykov (KAZ) 61 75.

China, P.R. relegated to Asia/Oceania Zone Group II in 2008.

Europe/Africa Zone
First Round 9-11 February

Israel defeated Luxembourg 5-0, Ramat Hasharon, ISR, Hard (I): Noam Okun (ISR) d. Gilles Kremer (LUX) 60 60 61; Dudi Sela (ISR) d. Gilles Muller (LUX) 46 64 62 76(1); Jonathan Erlich/Andy Ram (ISR) d. Laurent Bram/Mike Scheidweiler (LUX) 76(5) 60 63; Andy Ram (ISR) d. Laurent Bram (LUX) 62 57 64; Dudi Sela (ISR) d. Gilles Kremer (LUX) 64 75.

Georgia defeated Portugal 3-2, Tbilisi, GEO, Carpet (I): Irakli Labadze (GEO) d. Rui Machado (POR) 75 63 76(3); Lado Chikhladze (GEO) d. Frederico Gil (POR) 63 76(2) 67(3) 64; Lado Chikhladze/Irakli Labadze (GEO) d. Gastao Elias/Frederico Gil (POR) 76(6) 67(7) 76(4) 57 63; Pedro Sousa (POR) d. George Chantouria (GEO) 62 64; Gastao Elias (POR) d. George Khrikadze (GEO) 63 76(5).

Second Round 6-8 April

Slovak Republic defeated Macedonia, F.Y.R. 5-0, Skopje, MKD, Clay (O): Michal Mertinak (SVK) d. Lazar Magdincev (MKD) 63 62 46 64; Dominik Hrbaty (SVK) d. Predrag Rusevski (MKD) 62 63 63; Dominik Hrbaty/Michal Mertinak (SVK) d. Lazar Magdincev/Predrag Rusevski (MKD) 62 61 62; Pavol Cervenak (SVK) d. Ilija Martinoski (MKD) 63 64; Ivo Klec (SVK) d. Dimitar Grabuloski (MKD) 62 63.

Israel defeated Italy 3-2, Ramat Hasharon, ISR, Hard (O): Dudi Sela (ISR) d. Andreas Seppi (ITA) 63 75 16 36 63; Noam Okun (ISR) d. Simone Bolelli (ITA) 75 75 64; Jonathan Erlich/Andy Ram (ISR) d. Daniele Bracciali/Potito Starace (ITA) 63 76(4) 76(5); Andreas Seppi (ITA) d. Noam Okun (ISR) 76(4) 76(1); Simone Bolelli (ITA) d. Dudi Sela (ISR) 75 63.

Serbia defeated Georgia 5-0, Belgrade, SRB, Clay (I): Novak Djokovic (SRB) d. George Chantouria (GEO) 61 50 ret; Janko Tipsarevic (SRB) d. Lado Chikhladze (GEO) 64 64 75; Ilija Bozoljac/Nenad Zimonjic (SRB) d. Lado Chikhladze/George Khrikadze (GEO) 75 64 63; Ilija Bozoljac (SRB) d. Lado Chikhladze (GEO) 46 63 76(6); Janko Tipsarevic (SRB) d. George Khrikadze (GEO) 60 61.

Great Britain defeated Netherlands 4-1, Birmingham, GBR, Hard (I): Andy Murray (GBR) d. Raemon Sluiter (NED) 63 75 62; Tim Henman (GBR) d. Robin Haase (NED) 76(4) 63 76(4); Jamie Murray/Greg Rusedski (GBR) d. Robin Haase/Rogier Wassen (NED) 61 36 63 76(5); Robin Haase (NED) d. Jamie Murray (GBR) 46 76(0) 62; Tim Henman (GBR) d. Igor Sijsling (NED) 62 63.

Great Britain, Israel, Serbia and Slovak Republic advanced to World Group Play-offs on 21-23 September 2007.

First Round Relegation Play-off 20-22 July

Italy defeated Luxembourg 4-1, Alghero, ITA, Hard (O): Potito Starace (ITA) d. Laurent Bram (LUX) 61 63 64; Andreas Seppi (ITA) d. Gilles Muller (LUX) 61 61 64; Daniele Bracciali/Potito Starace (ITA) d. Gilles Muller/Mike Scheidweiler (LUX) 36 61 46 64 63; Gilles Kremer (LUX) d. Daniele Bracciali (ITA) 36 ret; Federico Luzzi (ITA) d. Laurent Bram (LUX) 64 64.

Second Round Relegation Play-offs 21-23 September

Macedonia, F.Y.R. defeated Luxembourg 3-2, Esch sur Alzette, LUX, Hard (I): Lazar Magdincev (MKD) d. Gilles Muller (LUX) 26 76(4) 63 16 63; Predrag Rusevski (MKD) d. Gilles Kremer (LUX) 64 36 63 57 64; Gilles Muller/Mike Scheidweiler (LUX) d. Lazar Magdincev/Predrag Rusevski (MKD) 67(4) 64 57 62 63; Gilles Muller (LUX) d. Ilija Martinoski (MKD) 63 64 63; Lazar Magdincev (MKD) d. Gilles Kremer (LUX) 61 63 67(1) 67(3) 64.

Netherlands defeated Portugal 5-0, Rotterdam, NED, Hard (I): Raemon Sluiter (NED) d. Frederico Gil (POR) 62 61 63; Robin Haase (NED) d. Gastao Elias (POR) 61 61 26 57 62; Jesse Huta-Galung/Peter Wessels (NED) d. Gastao Elias/Frederico Gil (POR) 62 67(5) 76(5) 63; Robin Haase (NED) d. Frederico Gil (POR) 63 64; Jesse Huta-Galung (NED) d. Rui Machado (POR) 63 36 62.

Luxembourg and Portugal relegated to Europe/Africa Zone Group II in 2008.

GROUP II

Americas Zone
First Round 9-11 February

Ecuador defeated Netherlands Antilles 5-0, Guayaquil, ECU, Clay (O): Carlos Avellan (ECU) d. Rasid Winklaar (AHO) 62 62 60; Julio-Cesar Campozano (ECU) d. Alexander Blom (AHO) 64 61 62; Carlos Avellan/Julio-Cesar Campozano (ECU) d. Raoul Behr/Nick Van Rosberg (ECU) 61 60 62; Jean-Michel Durango (ECU) d. Nick Van Rosberg (AHO) 63 60; Julio-Cesar Campozano (ECU) d. Rasid Winklaar (AHO) 64 75.

Uruguay defeated Jamaica 5-0, Punta del Este, URU, Clay (O): Marcel Felder (URU) d. Damion Johnson (JAM) 60 60 61; Pablo Cuevas (URU) d. Eldad Campbell (JAM) 61 61 62; Pablo Cuevas/Marcel Felder (URU) d. Elvis Henry/Jermaine Smith (JAM) 62 63 63; Martin Vilarrubi (URU) d. Damion Johnson (JAM) 61 64; Federico Sansonetti (URU) d. Eldad Campbell (JAM) 60 60.

Dominican Republic defeated El Salvador 4-1, Santo Domingo, DOM, Hard (O): Rafael Arevalo-Gonzalez (ESA) d. Henry Estrella (DOM) 76(4) 61 76(4); Victor Estrella (DOM) d. Marcelo Arevalo (ESA) 64 63 61; Henry Estrella/Victor Estrella (DOM) d. Marcelo Arevalo/Rafael Arevalo-Gonzalez (ESA) 76(0) 76(5) 76(2); Victor Estrella (DOM) d. Rafael Arevalo-Gonzalez (ESA) 75 41 ret; Jose Hernandez (DOM) d. Benito Jose Suriano (ESA) 61 63.

Paraguay defeated Cuba 5-0, Great Asuncion, PAR, Clay (O): Gustavo Ramirez (PAR) d. Edgar Hernandez-Perez (CUB) 63 75 16 60; Ramon Delgado (PAR) d. Favel-Antonio Freyre-Perdomo (CUB) 61 60 61; Emilio Baez-Britez/Ramon Delgado (PAR) d. Luis-Javier Cuellar-Contreras/Sandor Martinez-Breijo (CUB) 76(3) 76(3) 61; Juan-Carlos Ramirez (PAR) d. Edgar Hernandez-Perez (CUB) 75 76(5); Gustavo Ramirez (PAR) d. Favel-Antonio Freyre-Perdomo (CUB) 75 64.

Second Round 6-8 April

Uruguay defeated Ecuador 5-0, Punta del Este, URU, Clay (O): Marcel Felder (URU) d. Carlos Avellan (ECU) 63 61 63; Pablo Cuevas (URU) d. Julio-Cesar Campozano (ECU) 76(11) 63 63; Marcel Felder/Martin Vilarrubi (URU) d. Carlos Avellan/Jean-Michel Durango (ECU) 57 63 76(2) 60; Pablo Cuevas (URU) d. Jean-Michel Durango (ECU) 61 62; Federico Sansonetti (URU) d. Patricio Alvarado (ECU) 63 64.

Paraguay defeated Dominican Republic 4-1, Lambare, PAR, Clay (O): Ramon Delgado (PAR) d. Henry Estrella (DOM) 60 60 61; Victor Estrella (DOM) d. Gustavo Ramirez (PAR) 64 63 16 57 75; Ramon Delgado/Francisco Rodriguez (PAR) d. Henry Estrella/Victor Estrella (DOM) 64 46 61 32 ret; Ramon Delgado (PAR) d. Luis Delgado (DOM) 60 60 60; Emilio Baez-Britez (PAR) d. Henry Estrella (DOM) 60 62.

Third Round 21-23 September

Uruguay defeated Paraguay 3-0, Great Asuncion, PAR, Clay (O): Marcel Felder (URU) d. Gustavo Ramirez (PAR) 61 61 62; Pablo Cuevas (URU) d. Emilio Baez-Britez (PAR) 60 62 62; Pablo Cuevas/Marcel Felder (URU) d. Emilio Baez-Britez/Juan-Enrique Crosa (PAR) 62 64 62; final two rubbers not played.

Uruguay promoted to Americas Zone Group I in 2008.

Relegation Play-offs 6-8 April

Netherlands Antilles defeated Jamaica 5-0, Kingston, JAM, Hard (O): Jean-Julien Rojer (AHO) d. Damion Johnson (JAM) 61 62 62; Rasid Winklaar (AHO) d. Ryan Russell (JAM) 36 76(3) 62 62; Raoul Behr/Jean-Julien Rojer (AHO) d. Damion Johnson/Ryan Russell (JAM) 76(7) 76(5) 76(5); Nick Van Rosberg (AHO) d. Eldad Campbell (JAM) 46 61 64; Rasid Winklaar (AHO) d. Damion Johnson (JAM) 64 36 43 ret.

El Salvador defeated Cuba 4-1, Santa Tecla, ESA, Clay (O): Rafael Arevalo-Gonzalez (ESA) d. Luis-Javier Cuellar-Contreras (CUB) 61 57 64 63; Edgar Hernandez-Perez (CUB) d. Marcelo Arevalo (ESA) 64 36 64 20 ret; Marcelo Arevalo/Rafael Arevalo-Gonzalez (ESA) d. Luis-Javier Cuellar-Contreras/Sandor Martinez-Breijo (CUB) 64 75 61; Rafael Arevalo-Gonzalez (ESA) d. Edgar Hernandez-Perez (CUB) 60 63 61; Benito Jose Suriano (ESA) d. Sandor Martinez-Breijo (CUB) 64 26 76(2).

Cuba and Jamaica relegated to Americas Zone Group III in 2008.

Asia/Oceania Zone
First Round 9-11 February

Philippines defeated Pakistan 4-1, Manila, PHI, Hard (O): Cecil Mamiit (PHI) d. Jalil Khan (PAK) 61 60 61; Aqeel Khan (PAK) d. Eric Taino (PHI) 64 06 76(1) 75; Cecil Mamiit/Eric Taino (PHI) d. Aqeel Khan/Asim Shafik (PAK) 57 64 61 63; Cecil Mamiit (PHI) d. Aqeel Khan (PAK) 61 63 62; Patrick-John Tierro (PHI) d. Yasir Khan (PAK) 63 60.

New Zealand defeated Pacific Oceania 5-0, Dunedin, NZL, Carpet (I): Daniel King-Turner (NZL) d. West Nott (POC) 63 64 64; Simon Rea (NZL) d. Michael Leong (POC) 63 62 62; Daniel King-Turner/Simon Rea (NZL) d. Juan Sebastien Langton/Michael Leong (POC) 61 63 63; Jose Statham (NZL) d. Juan Sebastien Langton (POC) 76(4) 61; Adam Thompson (NZL) d. Brett Baudinet (POC) 62 67(1) 61.

Kuwait defeated Iran 4-1, Kuwait City, KUW, Hard (O): Ahmad Rabeea Muhammad (KUW) d. Ashkan Shokoofi (IRI) 75 76(5) 61; Mohammad Ghareeb (KUW) d. Shahab Hassani-Nafez (IRI) 60 62 62; Mohammad Ghareeb/Mohammad-Khaliq Siddiq (KUW) d. Shahab Hassani-Nafez/Ashkan Shokoofi (IRI) 62 76(3) 64; Ashkan Shokoofi (IRI) d. Ali Ismaeel (KUW) 61 76(3); Ahmad Rabeea Muhammad (KUW) d. Shahab Hassani-Nafez (IRI) 63 63.

Indonesia defeated Hong Kong, China 3-2, Causeway Bay, HKG, Hard (O): Prima Simpatiaji (INA) d. Hiu-Tung Yu (HKG) 57 63 63 62; Wing Luen "Wayne" Wong (HKG) d. Elbert Sie (INA) 36 62 63 61; Christopher Rungkat/Suwandi Suwandi (INA) d. Wing Luen "Wayne" Wong/Hiu-Tung Yu (HKG) 64 64 60; Elbert Sie (INA) d. Henry So (HKG) 46 60 63 63; Michael Lai (HKG) d. Christopher Rungkat (INA) 76(5) 62.

Second Round 6-8 April

Philippines defeated New Zealand 4-1, Auckland, NZL, Carpet (O): Cecil Mamiit (PHI) d. Jose Statham (NZL) 64 64 64; Eric Taino (PHI) d. Simon Rea (NZL) 61 62 64; Cecil Mamiit/Eric Taino (PHI) d. Daniel King-Turner/Simon Rea (NZL) 57 76(2) 76(4) 62; Patrick-John Tierro (PHI) d. Matt Simpson (NZL) 63 26 62; Jose Statham (NZL) d. Johnny Arcilla (PHI) 62 64.

Kuwait defeated Indonesia 4-1, Meshref, KUW, Hard (O): Mohammad Ghareeb (KUW) d. Prima Simpatiaji (INA) 76(7) 75 75; Elbert Sie (INA) d. Ahmad Rabeea Muhammad (KUW) 63 61 60; Mohammad Ghareeb/Mohammad-Khaliq Siddiq (KUW) d. Suwandi Suwandi/Bonit Wiryawan (INA) 67(3) 26 62 63 63; Mohammad Ghareeb (KUW) d. Elbert Sie (INA) 61 61 63; Ahmad Rabeea Muhammad (KUW) d. Prima Simpatiaji (INA) 36 64 64.

Third Round 21-23 September

Philippines defeated Kuwait 5-0, Meshref, KUW, Hard (O): Cecil Mamiit (PHI) d. Ahmad Rabeea Muhammad (KUW) 63 60 60; Eric Taino (PHI) d. Mohammad Ghareeb (KUW) 62 63 76(5); Cecil Mamiit/Eric Taino (PHI) d. Mohammad Ghareeb/Mohammad-Khaliq Siddiq (KUW) 67(5) 60 62 26 61; Patrick-John Tierro (PHI) d. Ali Al Ghareeb (KUW) 63 61; Johnny Arcilla (PHI) d. Ahmad Rabeea Muhammad (KUW) 61 75.

Philippines promoted to Asia/Oceania Zone Group I in 2008.

Relegation Play-offs 6-8 April

Pacific Oceania defeated Pakistan 3-2, Apia, SAM, Hard (O): Aqeel Khan (PAK) d. Juan Sebastien Langton (POC) 63 63 26 62; Michael Leong (POC) d. Jalil Khan (PAK) 61 61 61; Aqeel Khan/Shahzad Khan (PAK) d. Brett Baudinet/West Nott (POC) 57 76(6) 67(5) 75 63; Michael Leong (POC) d. Aqeel Khan (PAK) 61 62 62; West Nott (POC) d. Jalil Khan (PAK) 61 60 60.

Hong Kong, China defeated Iran 3-2, Tehran, IRI, Clay (O): Michael Lai (HKG) d. Anoosha Shahgholi (IRI) 67(3) 64 62 46 63; Hiu-Tung Yu (HKG) d. Ashkan Shokoofi (IRI) 64 76(2) 75; Anoosha Shahgholi/Ashkan Shokoofi (IRI) d. Henry So/Hiu-Tung Yu (HKG) 63 64 62; Hiu-Tung Yu (HKG) d. Anoosha Shahgholi (IRI) 67(1) 62 63 64; Rouzbeh Kamran (IRI) d. Gilbert Wong (HKG) 61 62.

Iran and Pakistan relegated to Asia/Oceania Zone Group III in 2008.

Europe/Africa Zone
First Round 6-8 April

Morocco defeated Denmark 4-1, Agdal, MAR, Clay (O): Rabie Chaki (MAR) d. Frederik Nielsen (DEN) 64 62 63; Younes El Aynaoui (MAR) d. Rasmus Norby (DEN) 60 63 64; Frederik Nielsen/Rasmus Norby (DEN) d. Rabie Chaki/Mounir El Aarej (MAR) 46 62 76(6) 63; Younes El Aynaoui (MAR) d. Frederik Nielsen (DEN) 63 75 64; Rabie Chaki (MAR) d. Martin Pedersen (DEN) 63 46 64.

Slovenia defeated Estonia 3-2, Tallinn, EST, Carpet (I): Grega Zemlja (SLO) d. Jurgen Zopp (EST) 46 64 76(3) 63; Mait Kunnap (EST) d. Marko Tkalec (SLO) 76(5) 26 76(10) 76(5); Mait Kunnap/Jurgen Zopp (EST) d. Luka Gregorc/Grega Zemlja (SLO) 62 36 36 76(5) 64; Grega Zemlja (SLO) d. Mait Kunnap (EST) 63 62 36 67(2) 63; Luka Gregorc (SLO) d. Jurgen Zopp (EST) 64 75 62.

Greece defeated Ukraine 3-2, Ioannina, GRE, Clay (O): Sergiy Stakhovsky (UKR) d. Alexander Jakupovic (GRE) 63 61 62; Konstantinos Economidis (GRE) d. Sergei Bubka (UKR) 63 62 64; Sergiy Stakhovsky/Orest Tereshchuk (UKR) d. Konstantinos Economidis/Alexander Jakupovic (GRE) 61 64 76(4); Konstantinos Economidis (GRE) d. Sergiy Stakhovsky (UKR) 36 62 36 64 63; Alexander Jakupovic (GRE) d. Oleksandr Dolgopolov (UKR) 76(3) 63 75.

Poland defeated Nigeria 5-0, Abuja, NGR, Hard (O): Lukasz Kubot (POL) d. Jonathan Igbinovia (NGR) 63 62 76(4); Dawid Olejniczak (POL) d. Abdul-Mumin Babalola (NGR) 61 64 63; Mariusz Fyrstenberg/Marcin Matkowski (POL) d. Abdul-Mumin Babalola/Jonathan Igbinovia (NGR) 76(4) 75 46 61; Mariusz Fyrstenberg (POL) d. Abdul-Mumin Babalola (NGR) 64 64; Dawid Olejniczak (POL) d. Jonathan Igbinovia (NGR) 63 26 63.

Latvia defeated Bulgaria 4-1, Jurmala, LAT, Carpet (I): Andis Juska (LAT) d. Todor Enev (BUL) 67(5) 63 63 76(3); Ernests Gulbis (LAT) d. Ivaylo Traykov (BUL) 63 62 63; Ernests Gulbis/Deniss Pavlovs (LAT) d. Ilia Kushev/Ivaylo Traykov (BUL) 75 64 62; Deniss Pavlovs (LAT) d. Yordan Kanev (BUL) 63 61; Ivaylo Traykov (BUL) d. Richards Emulins (LAT) 62 75.

Finland defeated Cyprus 3-2, Nicosia, CYP, Clay (O): Marcos Baghdatis (CYP) d. Juho Paukku (FIN) 63 63 76(3); Jarkko Nieminen (FIN) d. Photos Kallias (CYP) 61 63 61; Tuomas Ketola/Jarkko Nieminen (FIN) d. Marcos Baghdatis/Photos Kallias (CYP) 46 76(6) 62 63; Marcos Baghdatis (CYP) d. Jarkko Nieminen (FIN) 62 64 63; Timo Nieminen (FIN) d. Photos Kallias (CYP) 26 62 60 61.

Monaco defeated Algeria 5-0, Algiers, ALG, Clay (O): Benjamin Balleret (MON) d. Abdel-Hak Hameurlaine (ALG) 63 62 62; Jean-Rene Lisnard (MON) d. Slimane Saoudi (ALG) 75 64 64; Guillaume Couillard/Jean-Rene Lisnard (MON) d. Abdel-Hak Hameurlaine/Slimane Saoudi (ALG) 63 75 67(6) 62; Benjamin Balleret (MON) d. Mohamed-Redha Ouahab (ALG) 61 61; Guillaume Couillard (MON) d. Mehdi Bouabbane (ALG) 60 62.

Hungary defeated Norway 4-1, Oslo, NOR, Hard (I): Kornel Bardoczky (HUN) d. Frederik Sletting-Johnsen (NOR) 46 76(5) 62 75; Sebo Kiss (HUN) d. Stian Boretti (NOR) 76(5) 62 16 36 61; Kornel Bardoczky/Gergely Kisgyorgy (HUN) d. Stian Boretti/Frederik Sletting-Johnsen (NOR) 46 76(5) 76(4) 62; Adam Kellner (HUN) d. Philip Riise-Hansen (NOR) 62 64; Frederik Sletting-Johnsen (NOR) d. Sebo Kiss (HUN) 64 46 62.

Second Round 20-22 July

Morocco defeated Slovenia 3-2, Portoroz, SLO, Hard (O): Marko Tkalec (SLO) d. Rabie Chaki (MAR) 63 76(1) 76(5); Younes El Aynaoui (MAR) d. Luka Gregorc (SLO) 76(1) 64 63; Luka Gregorc/Grega Zemlja (SLO) d. Reda El Amrani/Younes El Aynaoui (MAR) 67(2) 64 64 64; Younes El Aynaoui (MAR) d. Grega Zemlja (SLO) 76(2) 62 64; Rabie Chaki (MAR) d. Luka Gregorc (SLO) 64 64 64.

Poland defeated Greece 5-0, Thessaloniki, GRE, Clay (O): Michal Przysiezny (POL) d. Konstantinos Economidis (GRE) 63 36 64 63; Lukasz Kubot (POL) d. Paris Gemouchidis (GRE) 62 60 62; Mariusz Fyrstenberg/Marcin Matkowski (POL) d. Elefterios Alexiou/Paris Gemouchidis (GRE) 64 60 61; Marcin Matkowski (POL) d. Elefterios Alexiou (GRE) 61 62; Mariusz Fyrstenberg (POL) d. Paris Gemouchidis (GRE) 62 64.

Latvia defeated Finland 3-2, Tampere, FIN, Clay (O): Ernests Gulbis (LAT) d. Juho Paukku (FIN) 75 61 62; Jarkko Nieminen (FIN) d. Andis Juska (LAT) 61 76(3) 62; Ernests Gulbis/Deniss Pavlovs (LAT) d. Tuomas Ketola/Jarkko Nieminen (FIN) 62 64 63; Ernests Gulbis (LAT) d. Timo Nieminen (FIN) 61 64 46 62; Juho Paukku (FIN) d. Karlis Lejnieks (LAT) 61 64.

Monaco defeated Hungary 4-1, Budapest, HUN, Clay (O): Benjamin Balleret (MON) d. Sebo Kiss (HUN) 61 63 63; Jean-Rene Lisnard (MON) d. Kornel Bardoczky (HUN) 61 36 76(1) 64; Kornel Bardoczky/Sebo Kiss (HUN) d. Guillaume Couillard/Jean-Rene Lisnard (MON) 61 57 46 64 62; Benjamin Balleret (MON) d. Kornel Bardoczky (HUN) 67(5) 57 64 60 60; Jean-Rene Lisnard (MON) d. Adam Kellner (HUN) 64 62.

Third Round 21-23 September

Poland defeated Morocco 4-1, Puszczykowo, POL, Carpet (I): Michal Przysiezny (POL) d. Mounir El Aarej (MAR) 62 64 61; Rabie Chaki (MAR) d. Dawid Olejniczak (POL) 46 76(3) 76(3) 67(4) 119; Mariusz Fyrstenberg/Marcin Matkowski (POL) d. Reda El Amrani/Mehdi Ziadi (MAR) 63 64 62; Michal Przysiezny (POL) d. Rabie Chaki (MAR) 62 64 64; Marcin Matkowski (POL) d. Reda El Amrani (MAR) 61 64.

Latvia defeated Monaco 5-0, Jurmala, LAT, Carpet (I): Ernests Gulbis (LAT) d. Jean-Rene Lisnard (MON) 61 ret; Andis Juska (LAT) d. Benjamin Balleret (MON) 64 64 75; Ernests Gulbis/Deniss Pavlovs (LAT) d. Benjamin Balleret/Guillaume Couillard (MON) 36 75 63 75; Karlis Lejnieks (LAT) d. Benjamin Balleret (MON) 76(4) 62; Andis Juska (LAT) d. Guillaume Couillard (MON) 46 63 62.

Latvia and Poland promoted to Europe/Africa Zone Group I in 2008.

Relegation Play-offs 20-22 July

Denmark defeated Estonia 3-0, Hornbaek, DEN, Hard (O): Frederik Nielsen (DEN) d. Mait Kunnap (EST) 62 62 76(5); Kenneth Carlsen (DEN) d. Jaak Poldma (EST) 76(10) 63 60; Kenneth Carlsen/Frederik Nielsen (DEN) d. Mait Kunnap/Alti Vahkal (EST) 64 62 64; Kenneth Carlsen (DEN) v. Mait Kunnap (EST) 75 23 play abandoned due to rain.

Ukraine defeated Nigeria 5-0, Lagos, NGR, Hard (O): Sergei Bubka (UKR) d. Abdul-Mumin Babalola (NGR) 61 64 62; Sergiy Stakhovsky (UKR) d. Jonathan Igbinovia (NGR) 62 60 63; Sergiy Stakhovsky/Orest Tereshchuk (UKR) d. Candy Idoko/Lawal Shehu (NGR) 63 62 64; Artem Smirnov (UKR) d. Candy Idoko (NGR) 63 62; Sergei Bubka (UKR) d. Lawal Shehu (NGR) 76(11) 26 62.

Cyprus defeated Bulgaria 4-1, Nicosia, CYP, Clay (O): Photos Kallias (CYP) d. Ivaylo Traykov (BUL) 76(2) 61 62; Marcos Baghdatis (CYP) d. Yordan Kanev (BUL) 62 62 62; Marcos Baghdatis/Photos Kallias (CYP) d. Todor Enev/Ilia Kushev (BUL) 62 63 63; Marcos Baghdatis (CYP) d. Todor Enev (BUL) 61 63; Yordan Kanev (BUL) d. Petros Baghdatis (CYP) 64 63.

Algeria defeated Norway 4-1, Svingvoll, NOR, Hard (O): Stian Boretti (NOR) d. Slimane Saoudi (ALG) 75 64 64; Lamine Ouahab (ALG) d. Erling Tveit (NOR) 64 63 60; Lamine Ouahab/Slimane Saoudi (ALG) d. Stian Boretti/Frederik Sletting-Johnsen (NOR) 62 26 75 62; Lamine Ouahab (ALG) d. Stian Boretti (NOR) 64 75 63; Slimane Saoudi (ALG) d. Frederik Sletting-Johnsen (NOR) 57 61 76(3).

Bulgaria, Estonia, Nigeria and Norway relegated to Europe/Africa Zone Group III in 2008.

GROUP III

Americas Zone

Date: 20-24 July **Venue:** Guatemala City, Guatemala **Surface:** Hard (O)
Group A: Bahamas, Barbados, Guatemala, Haiti
Group B: Bolivia, Costa Rica, Panama, Puerto Rico

Group A

20 June Bahamas defeated Haiti 3-0: Marvin Rolle (BAH) d. Jean Marc Bazanne (HAI) 61 63; Devin Mullings (BAH) d. Gael Gaetjens (HAI) 64 61; Bjorn Munroe/Marvin Rolle (BAH) d. Joel Allen/Jean Marc Bazanne (HAI) 64 63.

Guatemala defeated Barbados 3-0: Christian Saravia (GUA) d. Michael Date (BAR) 36 63 75; Cristian Paiz (GUA) d. Haydn Lewis (BAR) 57 61 63; Manuel Chavez/Sebastien Vidal (GUA) d. Akil Burgess/Russell Moseley (BAR) 64 76(4).

21 June Bahamas defeated Guatemala 3-0: Marvin Rolle (BAH) d. Christian Saravia (GUA) 63 61; Devin Mullings (BAH) d. Cristian Paiz (GUA) 61 62; Devin Mullings/Marvin Rolle (BAH) d. Manuel Chavez/Sebastien Vidal (GUA) 62 76(3).

Barbados defeated Haiti 3-0: Michael Date (BAR) d. Jean Marc Bazanne (HAI) 63 76(4); Haydn Lewis (BAR) d. Gael Gaetjens (HAI) 61 62; Haydn Lewis/Russell Moseley (BAR) d. Joel Allen/Gael Gaetjens (HAI) 76(4) 64.

22 June Bahamas defeated Barbados 2-1: Marvin Rolle (BAH) d. Michael Date (BAR) 60 62; Haydn Lewis (BAR) d. Devin Mullings (BAH) 63 76(5); Bjorn Munroe/Marvin Rolle (BAH) d. Haydn Lewis/Russell Moseley (BAR) 76(5) 46 86.

Guatemala defeated Haiti 3-0: Manuel Chavez (GUA) d. Joel Allen (HAI) 62 46 1210; Cristian Paiz (GUA) d. Gael Gaetjens (HAI) 61 21 ret; Cristian Paiz/Sebastien Vidal (GUA) d. Jerome Bartes/Jean Marc Bazanne (HAI) 61 64.

Group B

20 June Bolivia defeated Costa Rica 3-0: Mauricio Doria-Medina (BOL) d. Geoffrey Barton (CRC) 75 63; Mauricio Estivariz (BOL) d. Ignasi Roca (CRC) 75 62; Diego Camacho/Mauricio Estivariz (BOL) d. Rafael Brenes/Ignasi Roca (CRC) 75 67(3) 64.

Puerto Rico defeated Panama 3-0: Alex Llompart (PUR) d. Arnulfo Courtney (PAN) 61 20 ret; Gilberto Alvarez (PUR) d. Alberto Gonzalez (PAN) 63 46 62; Eduardo Pavia Suarez/Jose Emilio Sierra-Short (PUR) d. Augusto Alvarado/Juan Miguel Gonzalez (PAN) 57 75 61.

21 June Panama defeated Costa Rica 2-1: Geoffrey Barton (CRC) d. Juan Miguel Gonzalez (PAN) 76(4) 60; Alberto Gonzalez (PAN) d. Ignasi Roca (CRC) 61 60; Augusto Alvarado/Alberto Gonzalez (PAN) d. Rafael Brenes/Ignasi Roca (CRC) 67(7) 62 64.

Bolivia defeated Puerto Rico 3-0: Mauricio Doria-Medina (BOL) d. Alex Llompart (PUR) 62 61; Mauricio Estivariz (BOL) d. Gilberto Alvarez (PUR) 64 36 61; Diego Camacho/Mauricio Doria-Medina (BOL) d. Gilberto Alvarez/Alex Llompart (PUR) 76(5) 64.

22 June Puerto Rico defeated Costa Rica 2-1: Jose-Eduardo Pinto-Guardia (CRC) d. Eduardo Pavia Suarez (PUR) 67(5) 61 75; Gilberto Alvarez (PUR) d. Rafael Brenes (CRC) 64 63; Gilberto Alvarez/Alex Llompart (PUR) d. Geoffrey Barton/Ignasi Roca (CRC) 76(6) 63.

Bolivia defeated Panama 3-0: Diego Camacho (BOL) d. Juan Miguel Gonzalez (PAN) 60 60; Mauricio Doria-Medina (BOL) d. Alberto Gonzalez (PAN) 64 64; Diego Camacho/Mauricio Estivariz (BOL) d. Augusto Alvarado/Juan Miguel Gonzalez (PAN) 61 64.

Play-offs for 1st-4th Positions:

Results carried forward: **Bahamas defeated Guatemala 3-0; Bolivia defeated Puerto Rico 3-0.**

23 June Bahamas defeated Bolivia 2-1: Marvin Rolle (BAH) d. Mauricio Doria-Medina (BOL) 76(1) 62; Devin Mullings (BAH) d. Mauricio Estivariz (BOL) 62 62; Mauricio Doria-Medina/Mauricio Estivariz (BOL) d. Bjorn Munroe/H'Cone Thompson (BAH) 67(5) 61 75.

Puerto Rico defeated Guatemala 2-1: Alex Llompart (PUR) d. Sebestien Vidal (GUA) 64 75 64; Gilberto Alvarez (PUR) d. Cristian Paiz (GUA) 64 63; Manuel Chavez/Cristian Paiz (GUA) d. Eduardo Pavia Suarez/Jose Emilio Sierra-Short (PUR) 63 61.

24 June Bahamas defeated Puerto Rico 2-1: Marvin Rolle (BAH) d. Alex Llompart (PUR) 76(5) 62; Devin Mullings (BAH) d. Gilberto Alvarez (PUR) 62 75; Gilberto Alvarez/Alex Llompart (PUR) d. Bjorn Munroe/H'Cone Thompson (BAH) 46 76(4) 64.

Bolivia defeated Guatemala 2-0: Diego Camacho (BOL) d. Christian Saravia (GUA) 67(5) 62 63; Mauricio Doria-Medina (BOL) d. Cristian Paiz (GUA) 64 76(4); doubles not played.

Play-offs for 5th-8th Positions:

Results carried forward: **Barbados defeated Haiti 3-0; Panama defeated Costa Rica 2-1.**

23 June Barbados defeated Panama 3-0: Russell Moseley (BAR) d. Augusto Alvarado (PAN) 64 64; Haydn Lewis (BAR) d. Alberto Gonzalez (PAN) 64 63; Akil Burgess/Russell Moseley (BAR) d. Augusto Alvarado/Juan Miguel Gonzalez (PAN) 32 ret.

Haiti defeated Costa Rica 2-1: Jean Marc Bazanne (HAI) d. Geoffrey Barton (CRC) 61 63; Gael Gaetjens (HAI) d. Ignasi Roca (CRC) 63 26 61; Rafael Brenes/Jose-Eduardo Pinto-Guardia (CRC) d. Jerome Bartes/Jean Marc Bazanne (HAI) 76(5) 64.

24 June Costa Rica defeated Barbados 3-0: Jose-Eduardo Pinto-Guardia (CRC) d. Akil Burgess (BAR) 76(3) 45 ret; Geoffrey Barton (CRC) d. Russell Moseley (BAR) w/o; Rafael Brenes/Ignasi Roca (CRC) d. Akil Burgess/Michael Date (BAR) w/o.

Panama defeated Haiti 2-0: Juan Miguel Gonzalez (PAN) d. Joel Allen (HAI) 76(2) 16 119; Alberto Gonzalez (PAN) d. Gael Gaetjens (HAI) 64 76(5); doubles not played.

Final Positions: 1. Bahamas, 2. Bolivia, 3. Puerto Rico, 4. Guatemala, 5. Barbados, 6. Panama, 7. Costa Rica, 8. Haiti.

Bahamas and Bolivia promoted to Americas Zone Group II in 2008.
Costa Rica and Haiti relegated to Americas Zone Group IV in 2008.

Asia/Oceania Zone Group

Date: 16-22 July **Venue:** Colombo, Sri Lanka **Surface:** Hard (O)
Group A: Lebanon, Saudi Arabia, Singapore, United Arab Emirates
Group B: Malaysia, Oman, Sri Lanka, Vietnam

Group A

18 July Lebanon defeated Singapore 3-0: Karim Alayli (LIB) d. Min Wee (SIN) 62 63; Bassam Beidas (LIB) d. Chee-Jun Leong (SIN) 60 60; Bassam Beidas/Patrick Chucri (LIB) d. Daniel Heryanta Dewandaka/Min Wee (SIN) 61 62.

United Arab Emirates defeated Saudi Arabia 2-1: Mahmoud-Nader Al Balushi (UAE) d. Omar Al Thagib (KSA) 26 61 86; Omar Bahrouzyan-Awadhy (UAE) d. Fahad Al Saad (KSA) 67(1) 63 64; Saleh Al Raajeh/Tamer Antabi (KSA) d. Hamad Abbas/Faisal Bastaki (UAE) 62 61.

19 July Lebanon defeated United Arab Emirates 3-0: Karim Alayli (LIB) d. Mahmoud-Nader Al Balushi (UAE) 62 62; Bassam Beidas (LIB) d. Omar Bahrouzyan-Awadhy (UAE) 75 62; Bassam Beidas/Patrick Chucri (LIB) d. Hamad Abbas/Faisal Bastaki (UAE) 61 61.

Singapore defeated Saudi Arabia 2-1: Fahad Al Saad (KSA) d. Min Wee (SIN) 75 64; Chee-Jun Leong (SIN) d. Saleh Al Raajeh (KSA) 16 62 64; Daniel Heryanta Dewandaka/Min Wee (SIN) d. Saleh Al Raajeh/Fahad Al Saad (KSA) 76(3) 75.

20 July Lebanon defeated Saudi Arabia 2-1: Fahad Al Saad (KSA) d. Karim Alayli (LIB) 36 64 75; Bassam Beidas (LIB) d. Tamer Antabi (KSA) 75 61; Bassam Beidas/Patrick Chucri (LIB) d. Omar Al Thagib/Tamer Antabi (KSA) 61 76(3).

United Arab Emirates defeated Singapore 2-1: Min Wee (SIN) d. Mahmoud-Nader Al Balushi (UAE) 76(2) 63; Omar Bahrouzyan-Awadhy (UAE) d. Chee-Jun Leong (SIN) 64 61; Mahmoud-Nader Al Balushi/Omar Bahrouzyan-Awadhy (UAE) d. Daniel Heryanta Dewandaka/Min Wee (SIN) 63 75.

Group B

18 July Oman defeated Sri Lanka 2-1: Mohammed Al Nabhani (OMA) d. Renouk Wijemanne (SRI) 62 63; Harshana Godamanna (SRI) d. Khalid Al Nabhani (OMA) 62 63; Khalid Al Nabhani/Mohammed Al Nabhani (OMA) d. Harshana Godamanna/Rajeev Rajapakse (SRI) 63 64.

Vietnam defeated Malaysia 2-1: Minh-Quan Do (VIE) d. Qi-Hao Tan (MAS) 61 64; Yew-Ming Si (MAS) d. Quang-Huy Ngo (VIE) 62 36 62; Minh-Quan Do/Quoc-Khanh Le (VIE) d. Yew-Ming Si/Selvam Veerasingam (MAS) 63 64.

19 July Sri Lanka defeated Malaysia 2-1: Selvam Veerasingam (MAS) d. Renouk Wijemanne (SRI) 62 76(4); Harshana Godamanna (SRI) d. Yew-Ming Si (MAS) 62 64; Harshana Godamanna/Rajeev Rajapakse (SRI) d. Yew-Ming Si/Selvam Veerasingam (MAS) 67(4) 76(5) 62.

Oman defeated Vietnam 2-1: Minh-Quan Do (VIE) d. Mohammed Al Nabhani (OMA) 16 62 64; Khalid Al Nabhani (OMA) d. Quang-Huy Ngo (VIE) 36 75 63; Khalid Al Nabhani/Mohammed Al Nabhani (OMA) d. Minh-Quan Do/Quoc-Khanh Le (VIE) 26 75 63.

20 July Sri Lanka defeated Vietnam 2-1: Minh-Quan Do (VIE) d. Renouk Wijemanne (SRI) 61 36 62; Harshana Godamanna (SRI) d. Quang-Huy Ngo (VIE) 75 75; Harshana Godamanna/Rajeev Rajapakse (SRI) d. Minh-Quan Do/Quoc-Khanh Le (VIE) 63 64.

Oman defeated Malaysia 2-1: Mohammed Al Nabhani (OMA) d. Qi-Hao Tan (MAS) 60 60; Khalid Al Nabhani (OMA) d. Abdul-Hazli Bin Zainuddin (MAS) 61 76(2); Abdul-Hazli Bin Zainuddin/Qi-Hao Tan (MAS) d. Mohammed Al Nabhani/Suleiman Al Rawahi (OMA) 46 75 ret.

Play-offs for 1st-4th Positions:

Results carried forward: **Oman defeated Sri Lanka 2-1; Lebanon defeated United Arab Emirates 3-0.**

21 July Lebanon defeated Oman 2-1: Karim Alayli (LIB) d. Mohammed Al Nabhani (OMA) 62 62; Bassam Beidas (LIB) d. Khalid Al Nabhani (OMA) 64 64; Khalid Al Nabhani/Mohammed Al Nabhani (OMA) d. Bassam Beidas/Patrick Chucri (LIB) 63 64.

Sri Lanka defeated United Arab Emirates 2-1: Hamad Abbas (UAE) d. Renouk Wijemanne (SRI) 62 61; Harshana Godamanna (SRI) d. Omar Bahrouzyan-Awadhy (UAE) 62 60; Harshana Godamanna/Rajeev Rajapakse (SRI) d. Mahmoud-Nader Al Balushi/Omar Bahrouzyan-Awadhy (UAE) 63 61.

22 July Sri Lanka defeated Lebanon 2-1: Karim Alayli (LIB) d. Rajeev Rajapakse (SRI) 75 36 61; Harshana Godamanna (SRI) d. Rami Osman (LIB) 60 60; Harshana Godamanna/Rajeev Rajapakse (SRI) d. Bassam Beidas/Patrick Chucri (LIB) 62 63.

Oman defeated United Arab Emirates 3-0: Mohammed Al Nabhani (OMA) d. Mahmoud-Nader Al Balushi (UAE) 64 61; Khalid Al Nabhani (OMA) d. Omar Bahrouzyan-Awadhy (UAE) 64 36 31 ret; Khalid Al Nabhani/Mohammed Al Nabhani (OMA) d. Hamad Abbas/Faisal Bastaki (UAE) 61 62.

Play-offs for 5th-8th Positions:

Results carried forward: **Vietnam defeated Malaysia 2-1; Singapore defeated Saudi Arabia 2-1.**

21 July Vietnam defeated Singapore 2-1: Quoc-Khanh Le (VIE) d. Abdul-Hakim Jamaludin (SIN) 60 76(6); Quang-Huy Ngo (VIE) d. Chee-Jun Leong (SIN) 63 61; Daniel Heryanta Dewandaka/Abdul-Hakim Jamaludin (SIN) d. Quoc-Khanh Le/Thanh-Hoang Tran (VIE) 75 61.

Malaysia defeated Saudi Arabia 2-1: Fahad Al Saad (KSA) d. Selvam Veerasingam (MAS) 67(5) 63 61; Yew-Ming Si (MAS) d. Tamer Antabi (KSA) 63 57 63; Yew-Ming Si/Selvam Veerasingam (MAS) d. Saleh Al Raajeh/Fahad Al Saad (KSA) 63 63.

22 July Malaysia defeated Singapore 3-0: Selvam Veerasingam (MAS) d. Abdul-Hakim Jamaludin (SIN) 64 63; Yew-Ming Si (MAS) d. Min Wee (SIN) 63 61; Abdul-Hazli Bin Zainuddin/Qi-Hao Tan (MAS) d. Abdul-Hakim Jamaludin/Chee-Jun Leong (SIN) 76(9) 60.

Vietnam defeated Saudi Arabia 2-1: Thanh-Hoang Tran (VIE) d. Omar Al Thagib (KSA) 26 62 61; Quang-Huy Ngo (VIE) d. Tamer Antabi (KSA) 61 26 86; Saleh Al Raajeh/Fahad Al Saad (KSA) d. Quang-Huy Ngo/Thanh-Hoang Tran (VIE) 10 ret.

Final Positions: 1. Oman, 2. Lebanon, 3. Sri Lanka, 4. United Arab Emirates, 5. Vietnam, 6. Malaysia, 7. Singapore, 8. Saudi Arabia.

Lebanon and Oman promoted to Asia/Oceania Zone Group II in 2008.
Saudi Arabia and Singapore relegated to Asia/Oceania Zone Group IV in 2008.

Europe/Africa Zone - Venue I

Date: 9-13 May **Venue:** Cairo, Egypt **Surface:** Clay (O)
Group A: Bosnia/Herzegovina, Ireland, Lithuania, Moldova
Group B: Egypt, Iceland, San Marino, Turkey

Group A

9 May Ireland defeated Lithuania 2-1: Conor Niland (IRL) d. Ricardas Berankis (LTU) 76(5) 60; Louk Sorensen (IRL) d. Gvidas Sabeckis (LTU) 60 62; Daniel Lencina-Ribes/Gvidas Sabeckis (LTU) d. John McGahon/Kevin Sorensen (IRL) 76(6) 76(2).

Moldova defeated Bosnia/Herzegovina 2-1: Roman Tudoreanu (MDA) d. Ugljesa Ostojic (BIH) 64 60; Andrei Ciumac (MDA) d. Aleksandar Maric (BIH) 62 63; Mirza Basic/Zlatan Kadric (BIH) d. Radu Albot/Evghenii Plugariov (MDA) 63 36 63.

10 May Lithuania defeated Bosnia/Herzegovina 2-1: Daniel Lencina-Ribes (LTU) d. Mirza Basic (BIH) 76(5) 61; Ricardas Berankis (LTU) d. Zlatan Kadric (BIH) 61 76(4); Mirza Basic/Ugljesa Ostojic (BIH) d. Ricardas Berankis/Gvidas Sabeckis (LTU) 63 63.

Ireland defeated Moldova 3-0: Conor Niland (IRL) d. Radu Albot (MDA) 60 60; Louk Sorensen (IRL) d. Andrei Ciumac (MDA) 62 63; John McGahon/Kevin Sorensen (IRL) d. Radu Albot/Roman Tudoreanu (MDA) 63 61.

11 May Lithuania defeated Moldova 2-1: Daniel Lencina-Ribes (LTU) d. Roman Tudoreanu (MDA) 36 63 60; Ricardas Berankis (LTU) d. Andrei Ciumac (MDA) 64 60; Radu Albot/Evghenii Plugariov (MDA) d. Simas Kucas/Gvidas Sabeckis (LTU) 67(0) 64 63.

Ireland defeated Bosnia/Herzegovina 3-0: Conor Niland (IRL) d. Zlatan Kadric (BIH) 62 64; Louk Sorensen (IRL) d. Aleksandar Maric (BIH) 62 62; John McGahon/Kevin Sorensen (IRL) d. Mirza Basic/Ugljesa Ostojic (BIH) 63 64.

Group B

9 May Turkey defeated San Marino 3-0: Haluk Akkoyun (TUR) d. Domenico Vicini (SMR) 64 60; Marsel Ilhan (TUR) d. William Forcellini (SMR) 60 61; Haluk Akkoyun/Ergun Zorlu (TUR) d. William Forcellini/Domenico Vicini (SMR) 60 62.

Egypt defeated Iceland 3-0: Karim Maamoun (EGY) d. Andri Jonsson (ISL) 60 61; Mohammed Maamoun (EGY) d. Arnar Sigurdsson (ISL) 61 62; Karim Maamoun/Mohammed Maamoun (EGY) d. David Halldorsson/Arnar Sigurdsson (ISL) 64 60.

10 May Egypt defeated Turkey 2-1: Karim Maamoun (EGY) d. Marsel Ilhan (TUR) 64 63; Mohammed Maamoun (EGY) d. Ergun Zorlu (TUR) 63 75; Haluk Akkoyun/Ergun Zorlu (TUR) d. Karim Maamoun/Mohammed Maamoun (EGY) 46 62 64.

San Marino defeated Iceland 2-1: Domenico Vicini (SMR) d. Andri Jonsson (ISL) 60 60; Arnar Sigurdsson (ISL) d. William Forcellini (SMR) 61 64; William Forcellini/Domenico Vicini (SMR) d. Andri Jonsson/Arnar Sigurdsson (ISL) 64 76(5).

11 May Turkey defeated Iceland 2-1: Marsel Ilhan (TUR) d. Jon-Axel Jonsson (ISL) 60 60; Arnar Sigurdsson (ISL) d. Ergun Zorlu (TUR) 62 36 75; Alaatin-Bora Gerceker/Marsel Ilhan (TUR) d. Jon-Axel Jonsson/Arnar Sigurdsson (ISL) 60 64.

Egypt defeated San Marino 3-0: Omar Hedayet (EGY) d. Domenico Vicini (SMR) 61 63; Mohammed Maamoun (EGY) d. William Forcellini (SMR) 60 61; Omar Hedayet/Ahmed-Shebl Morsy (EGY) d. Vittorio Pellandra/Domenico Vicini (SMR) 21 ret.

Play-offs for 1st-4th Positions:

Results carried forward: **Egypt defeated Turkey 2-1; Ireland defeated Lithuania 2-1.**

12 May Lithuania defeated Turkey 2-1: Marsel Ilhan (TUR) d. Daniel Lencina-Ribes (LTU) 36 62 63; Ricardas Berankis (LTU) d. Ergun Zorlu (TUR) 60 76(3); Daniel Lencina-Ribes/Gvidas Sabeckis (LTU) d. Haluk Akkoyun/Ergun Zorlu (TUR) 62 76(3).

Ireland defeated Egypt 3-0: Conor Niland (IRL) d. Karim Maamoun (EGY) 64 61; Louk Sorensen (IRL) d. Mohammed Maamoun (EGY) 62 75; John McGahon/Kevin Sorensen (IRL) d. Karim Maamoun/Mohammed Maamoun (EGY) 67(3) 63 22 ret.

13 May Ireland defeated Turkey 2-1: Kevin Sorensen (IRL) d. Haluk Akkoyun (TUR) 64 76(5); Ergun Zorlu (TUR) d. John McGahon (IRL) 26 63 1311; John McGahon/Kevin Sorensen (IRL) d. Haluk Akkoyun/Ergun Zorlu (TUR) 76(8) 61.

Egypt defeated Lithuania 2-1: Karim Maamoun (EGY) d. Ricardas Berankis (LTU) 75 76(13); Mohammed Maamoun (EGY) d. Gvidas Sabeckis (LTU) 64 64; Simas Kucas/Daniel Lencina-Ribes (LTU) d. Omar Hedayet/Ahmed-Shebl Morsy (EGY) 76(5) 75.

Play-offs for 5th-8th Positions:

Results carried forward: **Moldova defeated Bosnia/Herzegovina 2-1; San Marino defeated Iceland 2-1.**

12 May Bosnia/Herzegovina defeated Iceland 3-0: Mirza Basic (BIH) d. Jon-Axel Jonsson (ISL) 61 61; Aleksandar Maric (BIH) d. Arnar Sigurdsson (ISL) 57 76(1) 75; Zlatan Kadric/Ugljesa Ostojic (BIH) d. David Halldorsson/Andri Jonsson (ISL) 62 61.

Moldova defeated San Marino 3-0: Radu Albot (MDA) d. Domenico Vicini (SMR) 75 67(6) 63; Roman Tudoreanu (MDA) d. William Forcellini (SMR) 62 62; Radu Albot/Andrei Ciumac (MDA) d. William Forcellini/Domenico Vicini (SMR) 21 ret.

13 May Bosnia/Herzegovina defeated San Marino 3-0: Ugljesa Ostojic (BIH) d. Domenico Vicini (SMR) 62 61; Aleksandar Maric (BIH) d. William Forcellini (SMR) 60 60; Zlatan Kadric/Ugljesa Ostojic (BIH) d. William Forcellini/Domenico Vicini (SMR) w/o.

Moldova defeated Iceland 2-1: Roman Tudoreanu (MDA) d. Andri Jonsson (ISL) 62 62; Andrei Ciumac (MDA) d. Jon-Axel Jonsson (ISL) 60 60; David Halldorsson/Arnar Sigurdsson (ISL) d. Andrei Ciumac/Roman Tudoreanu (MDA) 75 62.

Final Positions: 1. Ireland, 2. Egypt, 3. Lithuania, 4. Turkey, 5. Moldova, 6. Bosnia/Herzegovina, 7. San Marino, 8. Iceland.

Egypt and Ireland promoted to Europe/Africa Zone Group II in 2008.
Iceland and San Marino relegated to Europe/Africa Zone Group IV in 2008.

Europe/Africa Zone – Venue II

Date: 9-13 May **Venue:** Tunis, Tunisia **Surface:** Clay (O)
Group A: Cote D'Ivoire, Ghana, Mauritius, South Africa
Group B: Madagascar, Namibia, Tunisia, Zimbabwe

Group A

9 May South Africa defeated Mauritius 3-0: Fritz Wolmarans (RSA) d. Kamil Patel (MRI) 64 63; Rik De Voest (RSA) d. Jean-Marcel Bourgault Du Coudray (MRI) 62 63; Jeff Coetzee/Rik De Voest (RSA) d. Bruno Gorayah/Kamil Patel (MRI) 61 60.

Cote D'Ivoire defeated Ghana 3-0: Claude N'Goran (CIV) d. Menford Owusu (GHA) 61 63; Valentin Sanon (CIV) d. Mohammed Salifu (GHA) 60 57 61; Sylvain N'Yaba Lavry/Valentin Sanon (CIV) d. Emmanuel Mensah/Michael Nortey (GHA) 36 75 62.

10 May South Africa defeated Cote D'Ivoire 3-0: Fritz Wolmarans (RSA) d. Claude N'Goran (CIV) 61 63; Rik De Voest (RSA) d. Valentin Sanon (CIV) 63 61; Rik De Voest/Fritz Wolmarans (RSA) d. Claude N'Goran/Sylvain N'Yaba Lavry (CIV) 61 63.

Mauritius defeated Ghana 3-0: Kamil Patel (MRI) d. Menford Owusu (GHA) 26 61 64; Jean-Marcel Bourgault Du Coudray (MRI) d. Mohammed Salifu (GHA) 76(5) 16 63; Bruno Gorayah/Kamil Patel (MRI) d. Emmanuel Mensah/Michael Nortey (GHA) 63 67(2) 63.

11 May South Africa defeated Ghana 3-0: Fritz Wolmarans (RSA) d. Michael Nortey (GHA) 61 61; Wesley Moodie (RSA) d. Mohammed Salifu (GHA) 60 63; Rik De Voest/Fritz Wolmarans (RSA) d. Michael Nortey/Mohammed Salifu (GHA) 64 62.

Cote D'Ivoire defeated Mauritius 2-1: Claude N'Goran (CIV) d. Bruno Gorayah (MRI) 61 60; Valentin Sanon (CIV) d. Jean-Marcel Bourgault Du Coudray (MRI) 62 10 ret; Bruno Gorayah/Kamil Patel (MRI) d. Claude N'Goran/Sylvain N'Yaba Lavry (CIV) 61 60.

Group B

9 May Madagascar defeated Zimbabwe 3-0: Thierry Rajaobelina (MAD) d. Takanyi Garanganga (ZIM) 62 36 63; Tony Rajaobelina (MAD) d. Genius Chidzikwe (ZIM) 64 75; Germain Rasolondrazana/Jacob Rasolondrazana (MAD) d. Nigel Badza/Genius Chidzikwe (ZIM) 76(7) 61.

Tunisia defeated Namibia 3-0: Oualid Jallali (TUN) d. Johan Theron (NAM) 64 62; Malek Jaziri (TUN) d. Jurgens Strydom (NAM) 62 62; Oualid Jallali/Wael Kilani (TUN) d. Jean-Pierre Huish/Jurgens Strydom (NAM) 76(4) 60.

10 May Zimbabwe defeated Namibia 2-1: Takanyi Garanganga (ZIM) d. Johan Theron (NAM) 26 62 75; Genius Chidzikwe (ZIM) d. Jurgens Strydom (NAM) 36 63 62; Jean-Pierre Huish/Jurgens Strydom (NAM) d. Nigel Badza/Tinotenda Chanakira (ZIM) 62 76(11).

Tunisia defeated Madagascar 3-0: Oualid Jallali (TUN) d. Tony Rajaobelina (MAD) 76(6) 46 75; Malek Jaziri (TUN) d. Jacob Rasolondrazana (MAD) 61 62; Wael Kilani/Slah Mbarek (TUN) d. Thierry Rajaobelina/Germain Rasolondrazana (MAD) 60 62.

11 May Tunisia defeated Zimbabwe 3-0: Oualid Jallali (TUN) d. Takanyi Garanganga (ZIM) 62 67(2) 61; Malek Jaziri (TUN) d. Genius Chidzikwe (ZIM) 62 64; Wael Kilani/Slah Mbarek (TUN) d. Nigel Badza/Tinotenda Chanakira (ZIM) 62 76(11).

Madagascar defeated Namibia 3-0: Thierry Rajaobelina (MAD) d. Jean-Pierre Huish (NAM) 64 63; Jacob Rasolondrazana (MAD) d. Jurgens Strydom (NAM) 61 36 86; Tony Rajaobelina/Germain Rasolondrazana (MAD) d. Johan De Wit/Jean-Pierre Huish (NAM) 64 64.

Play-offs for 1st-4th Positions:

Results carried forward: **South Africa defeated Cote D'Ivoire 3-0; Tunisia defeated Madagascar 3-0.**

12 May South Africa defeated Tunisia 3-0: Wesley Moodie (RSA) d. Slah Mbarek (TUN) 63 62; Rik De Voest (RSA) d. Wael Kilani (TUN) 63 63; Jeff Coetzee/Fritz Wolmarans (RSA) d. Oualid Jallali/Slah Mbarek (TUN) 64 62.

Cote D'Ivoire defeated Madagascar 2-1: Thierry Rajaobelina (MAD) d. Claude N'Goran (CIV) 63 16 63; Valentin Sanon (CIV) d. Jacob Rasolondrazana (MAD) 26 63 61; Claude N'Goran/Valentin Sanon (CIV) d. Thierry Rajaobelina/Jacob Rasolondrazana (MAD) 62 63.

13 May South Africa defeated Madagascar 3-0: Wesley Moodie (RSA) d. Thierry Rajaobelina (MAD) 63 64; Rik De Voest (RSA) d. Jacob Rasolondrazana (MAD) 61 61; Jeff Coetzee/Fritz Wolmarans (RSA) d. Thierry Rajaobelina/Jacob Rasolondrazana (MAD) 61 60.

Tunisia defeated Cote D'Ivoire 3-0: Oualid Jallali (TUN) d. Sylvain N'Yaba Lavry (CIV) 62 64; Malek Jaziri (TUN) d. Valentin Sanon (CIV) 63 63; Wael Kilani/Slah Mbarek (TUN) d. Claude N'Goran/Sylvain N'Yaba Lavry (CIV) 30 ret.

Play-offs for 5th-8th Positions:

Results carried forward: **Zimbabwe defeated Namibia 2-1; Mauritius defeated Ghana 3-0.**

12 May Zimbabwe defeated Mauritius 3-0: Takanyi Garanganga (ZIM) d. Bruno Gorayah (MRI) 63 64; Genius Chidzikwe (ZIM) d. Kamil Patel (MRI) 62 26 61; Nigel Badza/Genius Chidzikwe (ZIM) d. Bruno Gorayah/Kamil Patel (MRI) 62 76(5).

Ghana defeated Namibia 3-0: Menford Owusu (GHA) d. Jean-Pierre Huish (NAM) 61 64; Mohammed Salifu (GHA) d. Jurgens Strydom (NAM) 67(3) 63 64; Emmanuel Mensah/Michael Nortey (GHA) d. Johan De Wit/Jean-Pierre Huish (NAM) 62 36 63.

13 May Ghana defeated Zimbabwe 2-1: Takanyi Garanganga (ZIM) d. Menford Owusu (GHA) 64 36 108; Mohammed Salifu (GHA) d. Genius Chidzikwe (ZIM) 63 62; Emmanuel Mensah/Mohammed Salifu (GHA) d. Genius Chidzikwe/Takanyi Garanganga (ZIM) 16 75 61.

Mauritius defeated Namibia 2-1: Kamil Patel (MRI) d. Jean-Pierre Huish (NAM) 60 61; Jurgens Strydom (NAM) d. Jean-Marcel Bourgault Du Coudray (MRI) 64 63; Jean-Marcel Bourgault Du Coudray/Kamil Patel (MRI) d. Jean-Pierre Huish/Jurgens Strydom (NAM) 64 63.

Final Positions: 1. South Africa, 2. Tunisia, 3. Cote D'Ivoire, 4. Madagascar, 5. Zimbabwe, 6. Ghana, 7. Mauritius, 8. Namibia.

**South Africa and Tunisia promoted to Europe/Africa Zone Group II in 2008.
Mauritius and Namibia relegated to Europe/Africa Zone Group IV in 2008.**

GROUP IV

Americas Zone

Date: 20-24 June **Venue:** Guatemala City, Guatemala **Surface:** Hard (O)
Nations: Aruba, Honduras, Trinidad & Tobago, US Virgin Islands

20 June Honduras defeated US Virgin Islands 2-1: Jose Moncada (HON) d. Eugene Highfield (ISV) 36 75 75; Calton Alvarez (HON) d. Kristopher Elien (ISV) 67(2) 61 64; Kristopher Elien/Eugene Highfield (ISV) d. Ricardo Lau Cooper/Jose Moncada (HON) 26 63 62.

Aruba defeated Trinidad & Tobago 2-1: Gian Hodgson (ARU) d. Brent Ching (TRI) 46 60 61; Clifford Giel (ARU) d. Richard Brown (TRI) 61 36 63; Brent Ching/Simeon Sealy (TRI) d. Sjoerd De Vries/Clifford Giel (ARU) 63 36 63.

21 June Aruba defeated Honduras 2-1: Jose Moncada (HON) d. Gian Hodgson (ARU) 76(3) 63; Clifford Giel (ARU) d. Calton Alvarez (HON) 64 75; Sjoerd De Vries/Clifford Giel (ARU) d. Pablo Costa/Jose Moncada (HON) 60 63.

US Virgin Islands defeated Trinidad & Tobago 2-1: Eugene Highfield (ISV) d. Simeon Sealy (TRI) 63 64; Kristopher Elien (ISV) d. Brent Ching (TRI) 64 63; Richard Brown/Lendl Smith (TRI) d. Eugene Highfield/Kevin Motta (ISV) 62 63.

22 June Honduras defeated Trinidad & Tobago 2-1: Jose Moncada (HON) d. Lendl Smith (TRI) 61 63; Richard Brown (TRI) d. Calton Alvarez (HON) 75 76(5); Calton Alvarez/Jose Moncada (HON) d. Brent Ching/Simeon Sealy (TRI) 60 60.

Aruba defeated US Virgin Islands 2-1: Gian Hodgson (ARU) d. Eugene Highfield (ISV) 62 64; Kristopher Elien (ISV) d. Clifford Giel (ARU) 63 63; Sjoerd De Vries/Clifford Giel (ARU) d. Kristopher Elien/Eugene Highfield (ISV) 63 57 75.

Final Positions: 1. Aruba, 2. Honduras, 3. US Virgin Islands, 4. Trinidad & Tobago

Aruba and Honduras promoted to Americas Zone Group III in 2008.